# THE ATLAS OF ANIMALS

## Linda Sonntag

### Consultant: Richard Walker B.Sc. Ph.D. P.G.C.E.

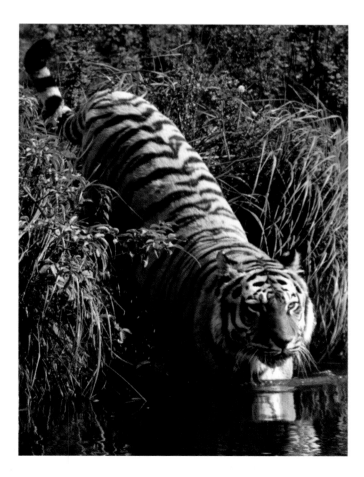

**Copper Beech Books**
Brookfield · Connecticut

© Aladdin Books Ltd 2000

*Produced by*
Aladdin Books Ltd
28 Percy Street
London W1P 0LD

*First published in the*
*United States in 2000 by*
Copper Beech Books,
an imprint of
The Millbrook Press
2 Old New Milford Road
Brookfield, Connecticut 06804

*Project Management*
SGA design & illustration agency
Hadleigh
Suffolk IP7 5AP

*Project Manager*
Philippa Jackaman (SGA)

*Designer*
Phil Kay

*Picture Research*
Brian Hunter Smart

*Illustrators*
Stephen Angel, Peter Barrett,
David Burroughs, James Field,
Karen Johnson, Ian Moores,
Stan Peach, Jonathon Pointer,
John Rignall, Terry Riley,
Chris Shields, Rob Shone,
Stephen Sweet, Michael Taylor,
Myke Taylor, Andrew Tewson,
George Thompson, Dan Woods

Printed in Belgium
All rights reserved

Library of Congress
Cataloging-in-Publication data

Sonntag, Linda.
    The atlas of animals/Linda Sonntag.
       p. cm.
    ISBN 0-7613-0925-X (lib. bdg.) --
    ISBN 0-7613-0845-8 (pbk.)
     1. Zoogeography--Juvenile literature.
     2. Habitat (Ecology)--Juvenile
     literature. [1. Habitat (Ecology) 2.
     Animal distribution.] I. Title

    QL101. .S65 2000
    590'.9--dc21

                  00-057011

*The author*, Linda Sonntag, has written
for children on a wide range of topics
including the living world, human
biology, and cultures and traditions
around the world.

*The consultant*, Richard Walker B.Sc.
Ph.D. P.G.C.E., trained originally as a
zoologist, and taught both secondary
school and university students before
becoming a writer and consultant.

# CONTENTS

# INTRODUCTION

Animals are found just about everywhere on Earth's surface: Across the continents of North and South America, Europe, Asia, Africa, and Australia, on islands, and in the oceans. But animals are not distributed evenly across the world. So why should some species (types) of animal live in one place but not others?

## Who lives where?

Each species has its favored habitat (place where it lives). Biologists divide the living world up into major habitats called biomes. Each continent has some, or all, of these biomes, which include coniferous forests, tropical rain forests, deciduous forests, grasslands, deserts, wetlands, mountains, and polar regions.

Biomes are shaped by climate—the average rainfall, the range of temperature, and the amount of sunlight they receive through the year. Climate determines which types of plant will grow in a biome. Because animals feed on plants—or feed on plant eaters—and because each species favors a particular climate, both climate and vegetation control which types of animal will live in a particular area. Animals are adapted to survive in their particular habitat. For that reason, similar biomes share animals with the same characteristics. The desert jerboa, for example, which lives in the Sahara Desert in Africa, is as perfectly adapted to hot, dry conditions as the very similar but distantly related kangaroo rat, which lives in North America's western deserts.

Niche

Population

Community

Ecosystem

## Biodiversity

Some biomes contain a much greater biodiversity—that is, many more species of animal—than others. Tropical rain forests, for example, have a much higher biodiversity than deserts. Being warm and wet all year round, forest conditions are ideal for plant growth, and the wide range of plants provides habitats and food for many animals. In the desert, only animals that can cope with heat, little water, and limited vegetation can survive.

## Lifestyles and living space

Wherever it lives, no animal exists on its own. Each animal species, or population, in a particular habitat interacts with others and with the surroundings. Different species survive in a particular habitat together because each has its own lifestyle, or niche, defined by its food, home, and way of behaving. The community of different species, together with their surroundings, form an ecosystem. Ecosystems can range in size from a pond to a complete biome. Together, all the world's ecosystems make up the biosphere—the life found in the air, on land, and in the oceans.

Biosphere

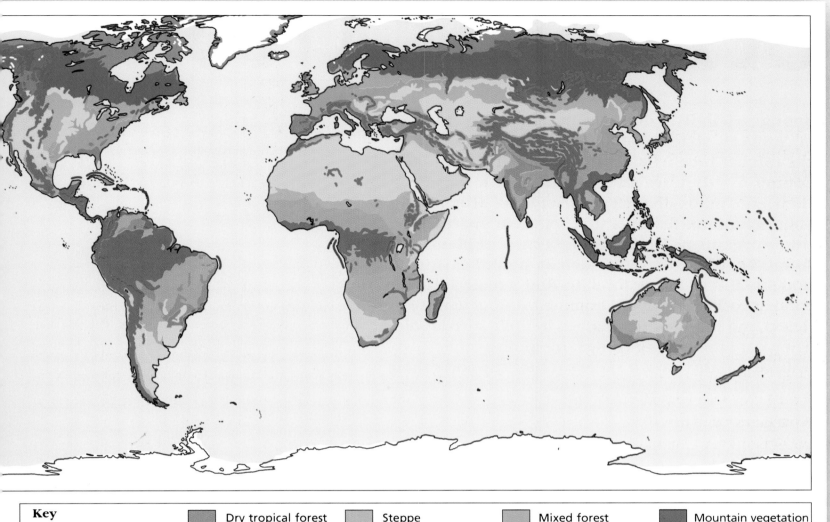

| Key | | | | |
|---|---|---|---|---|
| Desert | Dry tropical forest | Steppe | Mixed forest | Mountain vegetation |
| Dry tropical scrub | Monsoon forest | Prairie | Coniferous forest | Reefs |
| Subtropical forest | Tropical rain forest | Mediterranean scrub | Taiga (coniferous) | Icecaps and shelves |
| | Savanna | Deciduous forest | Tundra | Sea |

## Who eats what?

The link between animals in an ecosystem is "who eats what?" Animals eat in order to obtain energy to live. Sunlight energy is captured by plants, which are eaten by herbivores (plant eaters). These in turn are eaten by carnivores (meat eaters) that may be prey for larger carnivores. The route followed by energy as it flows from plant to animal to another animal is called a food chain. Because animals usually eat more than one type of food, food chains are linked together within an ecosystem into a complex food web.

## Human intervention

The fine balance in a food web can easily be upset by human intervention. The rapid growth of human population has resulted in damage to many habitats and ecosystems all over the world by, for example, hunting, cutting down forests to clear land for agriculture and building, and pollution. Many animals are now threatened with extinction, which means they may disappear forever.

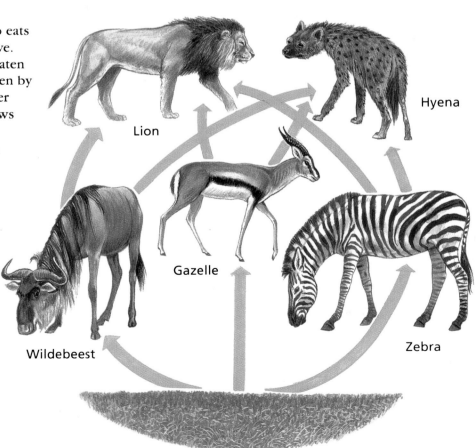

Lion

Hyena

Gazelle

Wildebeest

Zebra

5

# CLASSIFICATION

Sponges, jellyfish, dung beetles, lobsters, sea cucumbers, sharks, rattlesnakes, monkeys, and the mighty blue whale all have something in common—they are all types of animal. Despite their enormous diversity (variety), all animals share common features that set them apart from other organisms (living things) such as plants and fungi. They use senses—such as sight, hearing, and smell—to locate food, to find a mate so they can reproduce, to avoid enemies, and generally to detect and respond to changes in their surroundings. They eat other living things, including other animals. Many have a skeleton that supports their body and enables them to move.

## Numbers of animals

At the last count, over one million species, or types, of animal had been identified and described. Biologists believe that these represent only a fraction of the total number of species, and that there may be as many as 100 million different types of animal. Many of the species yet to be identified live in areas of high biodiversity, such as tropical forests and coral reefs. Unfortunately, these are the areas most at risk from human activities, so many of the unknown species may become extinct before they are even discovered.

## Naming and classifying animals

To make sense of the enormous variety of animals, biologists need an orderly method of naming and grouping them. The method they use is called classification, and it not only identifies and groups animals, it also shows how closely related animals are to each other.

Biologists classify animals by looking at their similarities and differences. Once this has been done, animals can be organized into groups of increasing size, from the smallest unit—the species—to the largest group—the kingdom—which contains all animals.

A species is a collection of similar animals—such as the lion—that are capable of breeding together in the wild. When an animal is identified as a species, it is given a two-part scientific name that comes from Latin or Greek. This system was created in the eighteenth century by Swedish botanist Carolus Linnaeus and is still used today.

o **Species**
*Panthera leo*, the lion, is like all other species—it is unique because of its individual features, and in the wild it breeds only with other lions and no other species.

o **Genus**
The lion and three other closely related big cat species are grouped together into the genus *Panthera*. All are hunters with slightly different lifestyles: The lion and leopard are found in Africa and Asia, the tiger in Asia, and the jaguar in Central and South America. The lion is the only social big cat and lives in groups called prides.

o **Family**
Genus *Panthera* is one of several related genera (the plural of genus) that make up the cat family (Felidae). All thirty-seven species of cat are lithe, active, mainly nocturnal (night) hunters that use their acute senses of sight and hearing to hunt prey. They live solely on meat or fish.

o **Order**
The cat family is one of eight families—the others are the dogs, bears, raccoons, weasels and otters, civets and genets, mongooses, and hyenas—that form the order Carnivora. Members of this order are mostly meat eaters that have sharp teeth and strong jaws. They either hunt prey or forage for carrion (dead animals). Some, like many bears, eat fruit as well as meat.

o **Class**
All the orders of mammal, including not only the Carnivora but also the rodents, primates (including humans), whales, and about twenty others, belong to the class Mammalia. Mammals are unlike any other animals because they have hair and feed their young on milk. They are also endothermic (warm-blooded), a characteristic they share with birds.

o **Phylum**
Mammals, along with birds, reptiles, amphibians, bony fish, and cartilaginous fish, belong to the phylum Chordata and are called chordates. Most chordates are known as vertebrates because they have a vertebral column (backbone).

o **Kingdom**
Finally, the many animal phyla (plural of phylum) —over thirty in all—make up the kingdom Animalia —the animals.

To find out how the classification system works, look at how the lion is classified as a member of the animal kingdom.

Lion
*Panthera leo*

Tiger
*Panthera tigris*

Lion
*Panthera leo*

Jaguar
*Panthera onca*

Leopard
*Panthera pardus*

Serval
*Eptailurus serval*

Cougar
*Puma concolor*

European wildcat
*Felis silvestris*

Spanish lynx
*Lynx lynx*

Lion
*Panthera leo*

Bobcat
*Lynx rufus*

Cheetah
*Acinonyx jubatus*

African wild dog
*Lycaon pictus*

Brown bear
*Ursus arctos*

Lion
*Panthera leo*

Meerkat
*Suricata suricatta*

Pine marten
*Martes martes*

Palm civet
*Paradoxurus hermaphroditus*

N. American raccoon
*Procyon lotor*

American beaver
*Castor canadensis*

Chimpanzee
*Pan troglodytes*

Common dolphin
*Delphinus delphis*

Lion
*Panthera leo*

Impala
*Aepyceros melampus*

Red kangaroo
*Macropus rufus*

Southern blossom bat
*Syconycteris australis*

Lion
*Panthera leo*

Harpy eagle
*Harpia harpyja*

Komodo dragon
*Varans komodoensis*

Edible frog
*Rana esculenta*

Clownfish
*Amphiprion percula*

Tiger shark
*Galeocerdo cuvieri*

Crown of thorns starfish
*Acanthaster planci*

Fiddler crab
*Uca pugilator*

Blue morpho butterfly
*Morpho retenor*

Octopus
*Octopus vulgaris*

Lion
*Panthera leo*

Portuguese man-of-war
*Physalia physalis*

Sponge
*Clathria sp.*

# ANIMAL KINGDOM

The animal kingdom is the largest of the five kingdoms of living organisms—the animals, plants, fungi, protists, and monerans. Perhaps the animals most familiar to people are the furry ones—mammals such as chimpanzees, rabbits, or pandas. Yet, of the million or so animal species, only about 4,000 are mammals. In fact, only a fraction of the total—about 45,000—are vertebrates (animals with backbones). The vast majority are invertebrates (animals without backbones). The largest group of invertebrates is the insects, a group that contains many species of beetle, not to mention all the other insect types. This classification of the animal kingdom is a "family tree" of related major phyla.

| *Porifera* (sponges) | *Cnidaria* (coelenterates) | *Platyhelminthes* (flatworms) | *Nematoda* (roundworms) | *Annelida* (segmented worms) | *Mollusca* (mollusks) |
| --- | --- | --- | --- | --- | --- |
|  |  |  |  |  |  |

## INVERTEBRATES

"Invertebrate" is a general term to describe the thirty-three out of thirty-four phyla of animals that are not vertebrates. Invertebrates are very diverse and, apart from not having a backbone, share few common features. The major invertebrate phyla include:

o **Sponges** (phylum Porifera—15,000 species)
Simple animals that live in the sea and freshwater, fixed in one place. They take in water through pores (openings), from which they filter out food.

o **Cnidarians** (phylum Cnidaria—9,000 species)
Soft-bodied animals, also called coelenterates, which live mostly in the sea. There are two forms: Polyps, which have a stalk at one end and a mouth at the other, and medusae, which have a mouth surrounded by a dome-shaped umbrella. Corals are built by polyps, while simple jellyfish are medusae. Large jellyfish are colonies of both polyps and medusae. Cnidarians catch small animals using stinging cells.

o **Flatworms** (phylum Platyhelminthes—20,000 species)
The simplest animal to have a distinct "head" region at the front of the body. They have a flat body and include free-living forms found in soil, water, and tropical forests, as well as parasites such as tapeworms.

o **Roundworms** (phylum Nematoda—12,000 species)
Also called nematodes, they have cylindrical, tapering bodies. Found in huge numbers in soil and sand. Also important parasites of animals and plants.

o **Annelids** (phylum Annelida—15,000 species)
Also called segmented worms, they have segmented, cylindrical bodies and well-developed body systems. Includes earthworms, marine ragworms, and leeches.

o **Mollusks** (phylum Mollusca—over 100,000 species)
Soft-bodied animals, many with a hard protective shell. Most, like snails, are slow-moving, but larger, more intelligent species, like squid, can move rapidly.

o **Arthropods** (phylum Arthropoda—up to 30 million species)
Largest and most successful animal group, they have jointed limbs and a body covered by a hard external skeleton. Includes insects (six legs), crustaceans such as crabs, and arachnids (eight legs) such as spiders and scorpions.

o **Echinoderms** (phylum Echinodermata—7,000 species)
Spiny-skinned, slow-moving animals with sucker-tipped tube feet, such as starfish and sea urchins.

*Mammalia* (mammals)

| Placental mammals | Monotremes (egg-laying mammals) | Marsupials (pouched mammals) |
| --- | --- | --- |
|  |  |  |

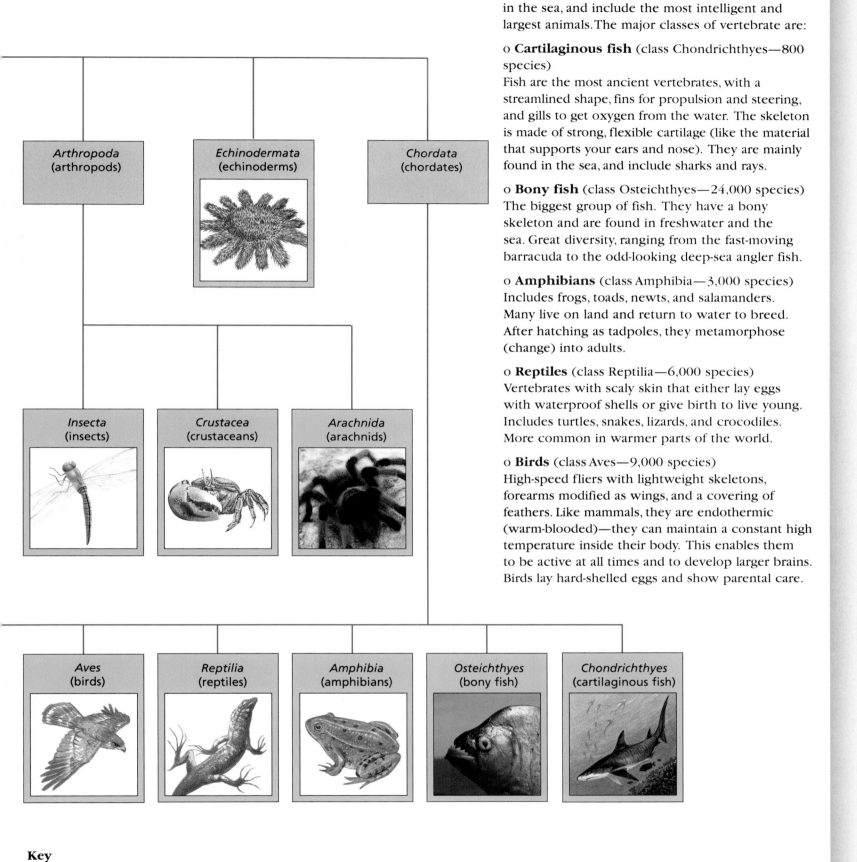

# VERTEBRATES

Vertebrates belong to the phylum Chordata and typically have a backbone, which forms part of an internal skeleton. They are found both on land and in the sea, and include the most intelligent and largest animals. The major classes of vertebrate are:

o **Cartilaginous fish** (class Chondrichthyes—800 species)
Fish are the most ancient vertebrates, with a streamlined shape, fins for propulsion and steering, and gills to get oxygen from the water. The skeleton is made of strong, flexible cartilage (like the material that supports your ears and nose). They are mainly found in the sea, and include sharks and rays.

o **Bony fish** (class Osteichthyes—24,000 species)
The biggest group of fish. They have a bony skeleton and are found in freshwater and the sea. Great diversity, ranging from the fast-moving barracuda to the odd-looking deep-sea angler fish.

o **Amphibians** (class Amphibia—3,000 species)
Includes frogs, toads, newts, and salamanders. Many live on land and return to water to breed. After hatching as tadpoles, they metamorphose (change) into adults.

o **Reptiles** (class Reptilia—6,000 species)
Vertebrates with scaly skin that either lay eggs with waterproof shells or give birth to live young. Includes turtles, snakes, lizards, and crocodiles. More common in warmer parts of the world.

o **Birds** (class Aves—9,000 species)
High-speed fliers with lightweight skeletons, forearms modified as wings, and a covering of feathers. Like mammals, they are endothermic (warm-blooded)—they can maintain a constant high temperature inside their body. This enables them to be active at all times and to develop larger brains. Birds lay hard-shelled eggs and show parental care.

**Key**

- Phylum
- Class
- Subclass

o **Mammals** (class Mammalia—4,000 species)
Mammals are endothermic (warm-blooded), have a covering of fur, and feed their young on milk. The majority—including whales, rodents, monkeys, and bats—are placental mammals that give birth to well-developed young. Marsupials, including kangaroos and opossums, give birth to tiny, underdeveloped young that grow inside a pouch. The three species of monotreme—two types of echidna and the platypus—lay eggs.

# ISLAND DIVERSITY

**The islands of the world contain a treasure store of animal species. Many island animals are endemic—that is, they are found nowhere else in the world. This is because, over millions of years, they have adapted and changed to suit their unique surroundings. Unfortunately, people have now wiped out animals that are irreplaceable by destroying habitats and introducing alien species. The Galápagos Islands and Madagascar show us how unique island animals are.**

The Galápagos are a group of volcanic islands in the Pacific Ocean, 620 miles (1,000 km) west of South America. All their wildlife arrived by flying, floating, or swimming from the mainland. The dominant land dwellers are reptiles, such as giant tortoises, lava lizards, and land iguanas, and birds, including the Galápagos finches. All are endemic to the islands. The wildlife has already been damaged by introduced species such as dogs, cats, pigs, and goats. Conservation is now a priority for the Galápagos, and tourism is strictly controlled.

Madagascar, the world's fourth-largest island, lies in the Indian Ocean, 250 miles (400 km) off the southeastern coast of Africa. Its mammals are all endemic, including the monkeylike lemurs. Its 257 reptiles—225 are endemic— include two-thirds of the world's chameleons. People arrived on the island some 2,500 years ago and began a process of habitat destruction, which has put much of Madagascar's remarkable wildlife at risk.

## Slowpoke

There are eleven subspecies of *Galápagos giant tortoise*—each has adapted to conditions on its particular island. The shells of those on dry islands are arched high above the creature's head, so it can stretch up to feed on prickly pear cacti. On more fertile islands, the tortoise's shell is lower at the front as it browses on low-growing plants. Giant tortoises can survive long periods without food and water and can live for over 100 years.

## GALÁPAGOS

## Sunbather

The *marine iguana* is the world's only sea lizard. It uses its powerful tail to propel itself through the water, and its legs to steer. Its sharp claws grip underwater rocks so that it can gnaw at the nutritious seaweed with its short, powerful jaws. Marine iguanas can be gray, green-brown, or pink and may grow up to 5 feet (1.5 m) in length.

## Woodworker

There are thirteen species of Galápagos finch. They look very similar, but their beaks differ slightly according to their diet. The ground finch has a strong, sharp bill for cracking seeds. The insect-eating warbler finch has a more delicate bill. The *woodpecker finch* has a long bill. This bird is unusual in that it uses a tool—a twig or a cactus spine—to dig grubs and insects out from under the bark of a tree.

## No escape

The Galápagos have the only *flightless cormorant* in the world. For centuries, the bird has had no predators to escape from, so its wings have lost the power of flight. It makes its nest of twigs and sea debris on the rocks and dives into the sea to catch fish. As its feathers are not waterproof, it holds out its wings to dry in the sun.

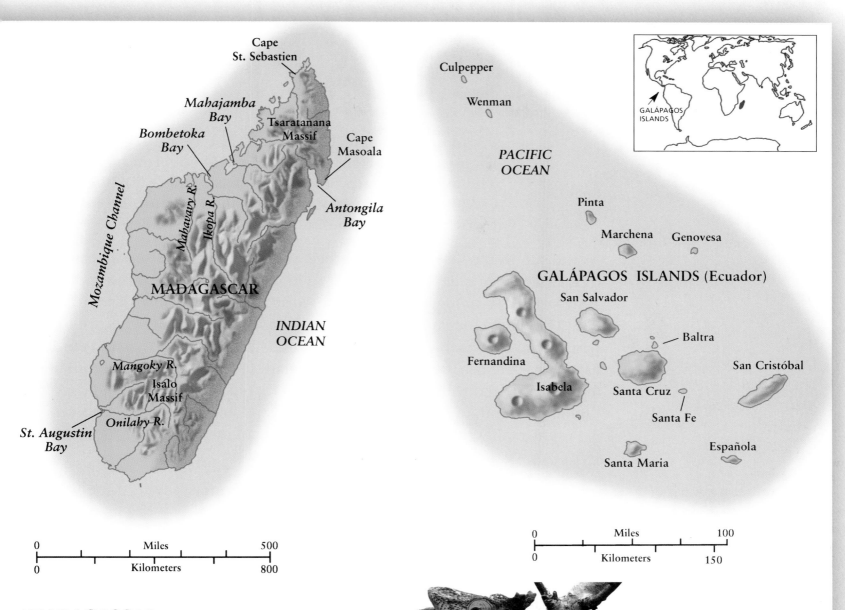

Cape
St. Sebastien

*Mahajamba Bay*

*Bombetoka Bay*

Tsaratanana
Massif

Cape
Masoala

*Mahavavy R.*

*Ikopa R.*

MADAGASCAR

*Antongila Bay*

*Mozambique Channel*

INDIAN
OCEAN

*Mangoky R.*

Isalo
Massif

*Onilahy R.*

*St. Augustin Bay*

| 0 | Miles | 500 |
| --- | --- | --- |
| 0 | Kilometers | 800 |

Culpepper

Wenman

PACIFIC
OCEAN

GALÁPAGOS
ISLANDS

Pinta

Marchena    Genovesa

GALÁPAGOS ISLANDS (Ecuador)

San Salvador

Baltra

Fernandina

San Cristóbal

Isabela

Santa Cruz

Santa Fe

Española

Santa Maria

| 0 | Miles | 100 |
| --- | --- | --- |
| 0 | Kilometers | 150 |

# MADAGASCAR

## Scent wand

*Ring-tailed lemurs* live in troops of up to forty animals in the sparse forests of the dry south of Madagascar. The females lead the troops, moving through the trees to feed on leaves, fruit, and bark. Troops also spend much time on the ground, walking on all fours with their tails erect, patrolling their territories. To mark its territory, the ring-tailed lemur uses scent from the glands under its tail. Rival males have "stink battles," waving their tails in the air like a wand.

## Hide-and-seek

The majority of the world's chameleons live on Madagascar. *Parson's chameleon* can change color through blue, green, brown, and yellow. Its skin has several layers of color cells, which are affected by its background, the level of light, and even its mood, such as fear or anger. Invisible to its insect prey, the chameleon grips a branch with its pincerlike feet, then shoots out its long tongue and catches its victim on the sticky tip.

## Long fingers

The cat-sized *aye-aye* is a type of lemur that leads a solitary life in the trees. During the day it sleeps in its nest, but at night it emerges to go in search of wood-boring insect larvae. The aye-aye taps on the bark of a tree, bites into it, then pries out grubs with its long, slender middle finger. Its large eyes help it see in the dark and its sensitive, batlike ears detect the rustle of insect prey. The aye-aye is now rare.

11

# THE OCEANS

**From space, Earth looks blue. The reason? More than three-quarters of its surface is covered by water. The average depth of the oceans is some 12,000 feet (3,700 m), and in places the seabed plummets into trenches nearly 36,000 feet (11,000 m) deep.**

As the sun shines, its rays are absorbed or reflected by the surface layers of the ocean. At a depth of 660 feet (200 m)—the bottom of the sunlit zone—there is no longer enough light available for tiny phytoplankton to use. They need the sun's energy to make food. These miniplants are the base of the food web. They are eaten by tiny zooplankton that, in turn, are eaten by small fish, which are eaten by sharks, seals, and whales. From 660 feet (200 m), the water becomes colder and colder and darker and darker until, at a depth of 3,300 feet (1,000 m), it is pitch black. There is, however, a remarkably rich diversity of marine animals at all levels of the ocean.

The coastal waters close to land are rich in fish, and are the areas exploited by commercial fishermen. Where these waters meet the land, a narrow strip—the seashore—has its own variety of animals living on sandy and rocky beaches, as well as in rock pools. These animals are adapted to survive being covered and uncovered by the tide.

The oceans have long been regarded as both an endless source of food and a vast dumping ground for human waste. It is now clear that overfishing, pollution by chemicals from agriculture and industry, radioactive waste, and oil spills are having a severe effect on life in the oceans.

## Jaws

The *great white shark* is feared as a killer in the oceans of the world. In fact, people are more deadly to the shark than it is to them, and the great white is now rare. Its torpedo shape and lightweight skeleton—made of gristly, flexible cartilage rather than bone—make the shark a fast swimmer. Its jaws have razor-sharp teeth about $2\frac{1}{2}$ inches (6 cm) long. The great white hunts seals, turtles, tuna, and squid, as well as other sharks.

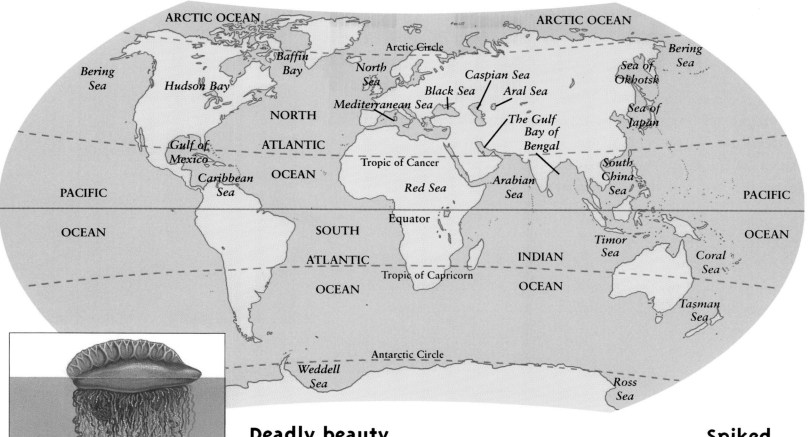

## Deadly beauty

The *Portuguese man-of-war* is actually a colony of tiny sea creatures called polyps. Each has a different function. The polyps form long tentacles that hang beneath a gas-filled float on the surface. Some tentacles bear stinging cells. When a fish brushes against them, these cells release poisonous barbs, which quickly kill the fish. The tentacles then lift the fish up to the float, where the polyps digest it.

## Spiked billfish

The *marlin*, with its streamlined body, sharply keeled fins, and powerful tail, is one of the fastest fish in the world. It cruises long distances in search of prey such as squid, mackerel, and tuna. In a school of fish, it strikes out with its spiked bill, then eats the dead and stunned fish. Because of its fearsome reputation, the marlin has become a common victim of "sport" fishing.

## Eight legs

The *octopus* lives in the rocks on the seabed. At dusk, it emerges to hunt shellfish. The octopus swims headfirst by squirting a jet of water backward through a funnel called a siphon. Well camouflaged, it ambushes its prey and stuns it with nerve poison. It can also squirt ink into the water to act as a screen. It grips its victim with its eight sucker-covered tentacles and drills through its shell with its saw-edged tongue.

## Caring father

The *seahorse* swims upright and feeds on plankton in shallow, warm waters. Its independently moving eyes can spot prey without it moving, and it can change color to suit its background. The female puts her eggs in a pouch on the male's abdomen, where he fertilizes them and carries the young until they are born.

## Musical crab

The male *fiddler crab* has a giant claw that he holds as if playing a violin. Fiddler crabs live on the world's warmer shores and dig burrows in the sand where they hide when the tide comes in. When the tide goes out, they feed by pushing sand and organic matter into their mouthparts. Females are quicker eaters as the males' claw, used for fighting and attracting a mate, is too big for feeding.

# THE ARCTIC

The Arctic surrounds the North Pole and includes the far north of North America, Asia, Europe, and much of Greenland. However, most of the Arctic is a massive sheet of ice floating on the Arctic Ocean. Conditions here are among the harshest on Earth.

In midwinter, it is dark twenty-four hours a day, the temperature drops to –58°F, and freezing winds blast the barren landscape. Despite this, many animals live here. Polar bears and Arctic foxes are active all year, hunting on the large, moving ice floes. Arctic hares and lemmings burrow into the snow to escape the winter weather. Other mammals and birds migrate—they leave to find food in warmer parts of the world, then return to breed during the brief Arctic summer.

With twenty-four-hour days, the ice sheet shrinks as temperatures rise. Snow melts to reveal the tundra—land where trees cannot grow and the lower soil is always frozen. The fifty days of summer are a time of rapid growth. Hardy, low-growing plants flower and attract nectar-feeding insects. Herbivores such as reindeer arrive, as do predators such as wolves. Both attract mosquitoes and other blood-sucking insects.

## Long-haul flight

The *Arctic tern* has the longest journey of any migratory bird. It breeds in the Arctic in the brief polar summer, then flies south for summer in the Antarctic—a round trip of nearly 20,000 miles (32,000 km) each year. This means that the bird lives in almost endless daylight. Arctic terns defend their nest and young by dive-bombing and hitting intruders, including humans.

## Snow bear

The *polar bear* is a powerful swimmer that hunts on the ice floes. Stalking its prey on the ice, it is camouflaged by its coat, and the hairy soles of its feet stop it from slipping. It eats seals, reindeer, rodents, fish, and dead whales. Polar bear cubs are born in dens dug in the snow. They are hairless, blind, and no bigger than rats, but in just four months they are ready for the outside world.

## Cold store

The fur of the *Arctic fox* is tawny in summer but turns white in winter to match its surroundings, so it can hunt and scavenge without being seen. Its thick coat, a layer of fat under the skin, and its furry paws help the Arctic fox survive the harsh winter, when temperatures plummet. To keep it going through the winter, the Arctic fox digs a cold store in summer, where it hoards dead animals and birds.

## Sociable migrants

*Snow geese* are not always white—they can be blue or gray. They fly north each spring to breed in the short Arctic summer, where they have virtually no predators or competitors. The birds nest on the marshy tundra in colonies of thousands. Snow geese pair for life and raise the young together. The goslings grow quickly and within a month are ready for the journey south to the marshlands of the Gulf of Mexico.

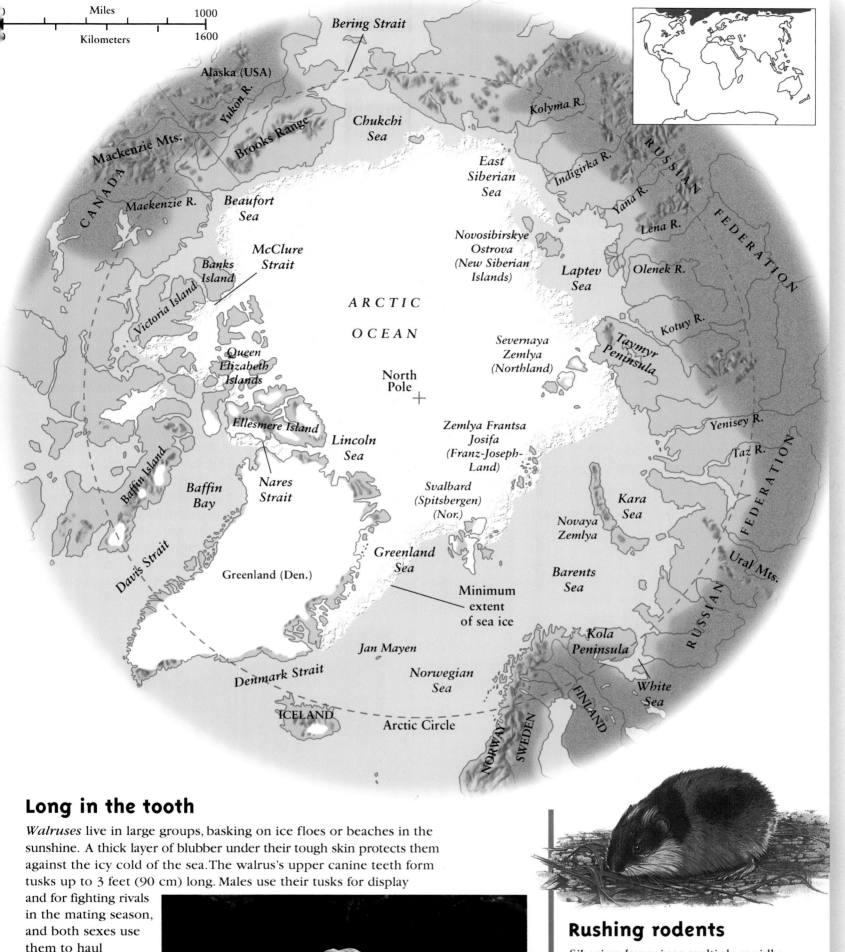

Miles 1000
Kilometers 1600

Bering Strait

Alaska (USA)

Yukon R.

Mackenzie Mts.

Brooks Range

Chukchi
Sea

Kolyma R.

CANADA

Mackenzie R.

Beaufort
Sea

East
Siberian
Sea

Indigirka R.

Yana R.

RUSSIAN

McClure
Strait

Banks
Island

Novosibirskye
Ostrova
(New Siberian
Islands)

Lena R.

FEDERATION

Victoria Island

ARCTIC

Laptev
Sea

Olenek R.

Queen
Elizabeth
Islands

OCEAN

Severnaya
Zemlya
(Northland)

Kotuy R.

Taymyr
Peninsula

Ellesmere Island

North
Pole
+

Baffin Island

Lincoln
Sea

Yenisey R.

Nares
Strait

Zemlya Frantsa
Josifa
(Franz-Joseph-
Land)

Taz R.

Baffin
Bay

Svalbard
(Spitsbergen)
(Nor.)

Kara
Sea

FEDERATION

Davis Strait

Greenland (Den.)

Greenland
Sea

Novaya
Zemlya

Ural Mts.

Minimum
extent
of sea ice

Barents
Sea

RUSSIAN

Jan Mayen

Kola
Peninsula

Denmark Strait

Norwegian
Sea

White
Sea

ICELAND

Arctic Circle

NORWAY

SWEDEN

FINLAND

## Long in the tooth

*Walruses* live in large groups, basking on ice floes or beaches in the sunshine. A thick layer of blubber under their tough skin protects them against the icy cold of the sea. The walrus's upper canine teeth form tusks up to 3 feet (90 cm) long. Males use their tusks for display and for fighting rivals in the mating season, and both sexes use them to haul themselves out of the water. Walruses feed on mollusks and other shellfish that they dig from the seabed with their strong, bristly snouts.

## Rushing rodents

*Siberian lemmings* multiply rapidly. They can mate at just two weeks old and have their first litter in a month. Every four years, there is a sudden population increase, so they migrate by the million in search of new food supplies. They leap gorges, swim rivers, and cross roads—behavior that has led to the myth that lemmings commit suicide.

# EUROPE

**Lying between the Atlantic and Arctic Oceans and the Mediterranean Sea, and stretching as far as the Urals, Europe is the world's second smallest continent after Australia. Attracted by the mild climate and rich, fertile soils, Europe's dense human population has greatly reduced the number of animals.**

Broad-leaved woodlands and forests once stretched across Europe in a band from the British Isles in the west to Russia in the east. In what is left of these, the wildlife is diverse and some large mammals, such as wolves and bears, remain. In the far north of Europe, where winters are long and cold, large areas of conifers are home to animals that can survive the harsh conditions, such as pine martens and wolves. Europe's mountains, the largest of which are the Alps and the Pyrenees, straddle Europe from west to east. They provide a natural barrier that protects the south from rain and cold winds. Southern Europe—around the Mediterranean Sea—basks in a warm, dry climate, where lizards and tortoises thrive. There are marshes and lakes throughout Europe, except where it is too cold or too dry, and rivers that wind down to the sea. Each wetland habitat has its own range of animals including frogs, fish, and water birds.

## Forests and mountains

Adult *European wildcat*s live alone, marking their territory with urine and scratch marks. They meet only in the breeding season, where several males may court one female, screeching and wailing all night. The female makes a nest in a rocky shelter or a hollow tree. When her kittens are three months old, they gradually learn to hunt rabbits, birds, and insects. At about six months, the young are ready to fend for themselves. The wildcat was once found all over Europe, but is now rare.

## Wetlands

The *Eurasian otter* lives by riverbanks and the seashore, and eats shellfish and fish. Its ears and nostrils close when it dives and its streamlined body allows it to move quickly through the water. Otters mark a territory with droppings called spraint. The young are born in a holt (burrow). The mother suckles them and drives the male away. They learn to swim at two months, but they may stay with her for a year. Numbers have been reduced by hunting, pesticides, and road kills.

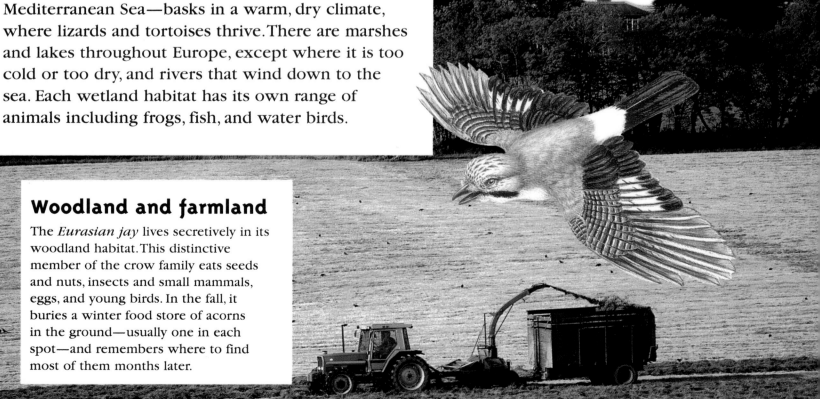

## Woodland and farmland

The *Eurasian jay* lives secretively in its woodland habitat. This distinctive member of the crow family eats seeds and nuts, insects and small mammals, eggs, and young birds. In the fall, it buries a winter food store of acorns in the ground—usually one in each spot—and remembers where to find most of them months later.

ICELAND

Barents Sea

Norwegian
Sea

Faröe
Islands
(Den.)

Shetland
Islands
(U.K.)

Orkney
Islands
(U.K.)

North
Sea

Kola
Peninsula

White Sea

Pechora R.

Ural Mts.

Dvina R.

L. Onega

NORWAY

SWEDEN

Gulf of Bothnia

FINLAND

L. Ladoga

RUSSIAN FEDERATION

L. Vänern

L. Vättern

Baltic Sea

ESTONIA

LATVIA

LITHUANIA

1

5

Ural R.

BELO-
RUSSIA

UNITED
KINGDOM

REPUBLIC
OF
IRELAND

Thames R.

2

GERMANY

POLAND

Vistula R.

UKRAINE

Don R.

Volga R.

English Channel

3

4

Rhine R.

CZECH
REPUBLIC

7

Carpathian Mts.

12

Dnieper R.

ATLANTIC
OCEAN

Seine R.

Loire R.

FRANCE

AUSTRIA

6

The Alps

HUNGARY

8

9

Sea of
Azov

Caucasus Mts.

Caspian Sea

Bay of
Biscay

Rhone R.

Po R.

ITALY

10

11

ROMANIA

Danube R.

Black Sea

Pyrenees Mts.

Corsica (Fr.)

Adriatic Sea

14

13

BULGARIA

PORTUGAL

Tagus R.

SPAIN

Sardinia (It.)

Balearic
Islands (Sp.)

GREECE

Aegean
Sea

Strait of
Gibraltar

Sicily (It.)

Mediterranean Sea

Crete (Gr.)

| | |
|---|---|
| 1 | DENMARK |
| 2 | NETHERLANDS |
| 3 | BELGIUM |
| 4 | LUXEMBOURG |
| 5 | RUSSIAN FEDERATION |
| 6 | SWITZERLAND |
| 7 | SLOVAKIA |
| 8 | SLOVENIA |
| 9 | CROATIA |
| 10 | BOSNIA-HERZEGOVINA |
| 11 | YUGOSLAVIA |
| 12 | MOLDOVA |
| 13 | MACEDONIA |
| 14 | ALBANIA |

| 0 | Miles | 1000 |
|---|---|---|
| 0 | Kilometers | 1600 |

## Southern Europe

The *brown bear* lives in the mountains of southern Europe. Its diet includes berries and nuts, roots, fish—such as salmon—and rodents. It has poor eyesight and relies on its sense of smell for hunting. Brown bears mate in summer, but the fertilized eggs do not implant in the mother's womb until the fall, so she has time to feed well and put on fat. The cubs are born in winter, in a cave or a den dug into a hillside. Here, the female sleeps through the cold months when food is scarce. When the bears emerge from their slumber in spring, the cubs learn to forage and hunt.

# FORESTS AND MOUNTAINS

Mountains
Forests

Europe's coniferous forests, made up of spruce, fir, and pine, can tolerate bitter winters and are spread across Scotland, Scandinavia, and Russia. The seeds of conifer pine cones provide a rich source of food for crossbills and squirrels. In the summer, the forests are alive with insects such as midges, and flies, which provide food for bats and insect-eating birds. Owls and golden eagles swoop down to eat birds, lizards, and small mammals. In winter, the days become shorter and colder. Many animals hibernate or migrate to warmer locations. Only the toughest carry on the search for food during winter.

The Carpathians, Alps, and Pyrenees, Europe's major mountains, sweep across the continent from east to west. With increasing altitude (height), the mountain climate changes and so do its vegetation and animals. It becomes colder and colder and also windier. The woodlands of the lower slopes give way to alpine meadows, above which are bare, snow-covered rocks. Only animals that can survive harsh conditions live here.

Surefooted larger mammals, such as mouflon and chamois, move with ease over steep and rocky terrain. Smaller mammals and birds thrive in the alpine meadows in summer, when flowering plants and insects provide food, while birds of prey soar in the air.

## FORESTS
### Fighting pig

The *wild boar* is the ancestor of the domestic pig. It has thick fur and uses its strong snout for digging up food. It eats roots, bulbs, and small animals. The males use their powerful head and tusks to fight each other when competing for females in the herd. A litter of up to twelve piglets is born in the spring. Unlike their parents, the piglets have striped fur to camouflage them within their surroundings.

### Cone cracker

*Crossbills* of the northern forests raise their chicks early in the year when there is plenty of food. They live on spruce cone seeds, which ripen during the winter and open in spring. The crossbill hangs upside down on a large cone, then uses the two halves of its crossed beak to force apart the scales so it can lick out the seed with its tongue. The adults partly digest the seeds then regurgitate them (bring them back up) to feed their young.

### Acid spray

*Wood ants* work together to build large nests of leaves, pine needles, and forest floor debris. In winter, they hibernate in the soil under the mound to keep warm. They feed on other insects. If threatened or disturbed, wood ants fire a stinging spray of formic acid to ward off their enemies.

# MOUNTAINS
## Acrobatic flight

The sociable *Alpine chough* is a member of the crow family that bonds strongly with its mate. Choughs live in large flocks and roost in caves or under rocky crags. In summer, they live high in the mountains, where their strong wings enable them to glide on air currents. In winter, they descend to the valleys. They feed on insects, snails, berries, and on the carcasses of small animals.

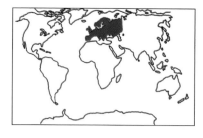

## Sociable burrower

The *Alpine marmot* is a relative of the squirrel which hibernates for half a year deep in its hay-lined burrow. Many families live close together, in burrows about 10 feet (3 m) deep. In the summer, they feed on grass, seeds, and fruits, building up vital fat reserves needed for their hibernation. Marmots begin to breed when they emerge from hibernation in the spring.

## Mountaineer

Soon after birth, a *chamois* can spring across the rocks. It has strong legs and pads under its hooves to help it grip and make leaps of up to 20 feet (6 m). Its speed and agility protect it from predatory wolves and bears. Chamois spend the summers grazing on high mountain meadows and the winters lower down in the woodlands, scratching around for shoots, mosses, and lichens to eat.

## Mole swimmer

The *Pyrenean desman* is related to the mole and lives near swiftly flowing streams. It has webbed feet and a long, flattened, rudderlike tail. It rests in its burrow in the riverbank by day and comes out at night to hunt for small fish, shellfish, insects, and worms. It is at risk from fishermen and the pollution of mountain streams.

## Endangered hunter

The *golden eagle* soars on air currents looking for small mammals, birds, lizards, and carrion. Swooping to the kill, the eagle crushes its prey with its talons, then rips it to bits with its sharp, hooked beak. Golden eagles nest on rocky ledges and usually lay two eggs. The first chick to hatch may kill its weaker sibling. In some areas, they are threatened by shooting, poisoning, and loss of habitat.

# WOODLAND AND FARMLAND

Woodland
Farmland

The European woodlands of broad-leaved trees are dominated by oak and beech trees, providing home, shelter, and food for a rich variety of animal life that changes with the seasons. In the fall, the trees lose their leaves as they prepare for winter. In spring, there is a rebirth: Buds, leaves, and flowers appear, turning the woods green. Insects hatch out to feed on the young leaves and suck sap from stems. In turn, the insects provide food for birds, such as treecreepers.

Mammals also start to breed in spring, when food supplies are available. Deer feed on grasses and flowers that appear in forest clearings, squirrels scramble up and down tree trunks as they forage for seeds and fruits, while foxes hunt for small prey such as mice. Fallen leaves on the forest floor provide a rich leaf litter that is home to many insects, and also nourishes the soil. During the warm summer months, young animals grow and become independent. By fall, as the leaves drop once again, the woods provide a feast of fruits, nuts, and fungi. Woodland animals gorge themselves to prepare for the cold months ahead.

Although much of Europe's woodland has been cut down, greatly reducing habitat, woodland animals still manage to survive in hedges and copses. Foxes and badgers roam in fields at night and harvest mice nest between stalks of wheat.

## Not so fierce

Male *stag beetles* have huge antler-shaped jaws, which they wave to attract a mate. If a rival comes along, they fight. One may even lift the other off the ground, but neither is injured—the loser runs away. The eggs are laid in the soft wood of a dead tree. The grubs hatch and live off the rotting wood for three years, before turning into adults. Their life as a beetle lasts only a month.

## Intensive farming

Modern intensive farming has severely reduced the variety of farmland life. Hedgerows have been plowed up, removing the natural home of wild birds that feed on insect pests. Pesticides are sprayed to control the insects that feed on crops, but also kill many useful insects, such as bees and ladybugs. To produce the highest crop yields, fertilizer is regularly added. Residues from the fertilizers run into rivers and lakes, causing water plants to grow out of control.

## Sensitive nose

The *European hedgehog* is covered in around 5,000 sharp spines. If threatened, it erects its spines by tensing muscles under the skin. If danger persists, it arches its body, tucks in its head, and rolls itself into a spiny ball. Hedgehogs hunt at night, sniffing out insects, worms, spiders, and snails. They feed well in the fall, laying on fat to keep them going through hibernation.

## Eurasian sparrowhawk

○ Flies swiftly on the lookout for prey.
○ Main prey—other birds, which it seizes in flight after a short, fast chase.
○ Takes its prey to a feeding post to pluck and eat it.
○ Lives in woodland and scrub.
○ Builds its nest in a tree.
○ Female is larger than the male, and is distinguished by the white spot on her nape.

## European mole

○ Lives underground in a system of tunnels with a food store close to the nest chamber.
○ Short, strong arms that it uses like spades for digging.
○ Main food—earthworms that fall into its tunnels. It bites off their "head" and keeps their body in its food store.
○ Poor senses of smell, hearing, and sight, but has an excellent sense of touch.

## Eurasian badger

○ Groups of up to fifteen animals in one underground sett (burrow).
○ Often clears out the sett and brings in fresh bedding.
○ Poor eyesight, it relies on smell to find food at night—small mammals, insects, slugs, frogs, roots, and plants.
○ A protected animal, but tragically, many are killed each year or meet with death on the roads.

## Common blue butterfly

○ Males have blue wings. Females have brown wings with orange edges.
○ Caterpillar's food plants are vetch, clover, trefoil, and other members of the pea family.
○ Adult butterflies sip the sweet nectar of wildflowers such as marjoram and thistle.
○ Groups of males drink from puddles to get the minerals they need to build their hormones.

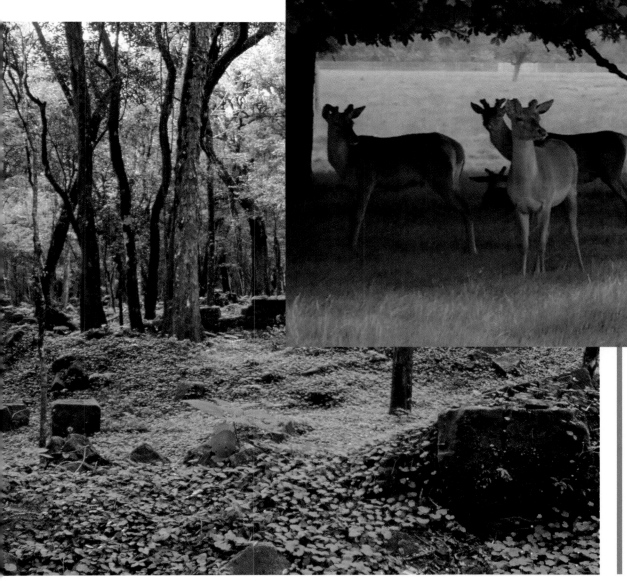

## Stags and hinds

During the rut (mating season), red deer stags roar and lock antlers, competing with each other for females, called hinds. A successful stag can mate with around forty hinds. After the rut, the stags leave to form bachelor groups. When the calves are born, their mothers hide them in a den, returning to suckle them until they can run with the herd.

21

# WETLANDS

## EUROPE

Europe's wetlands are found wherever land meets water. Pools, ponds, lakes, flooded areas next to rivers, swamps, and bogs—all are home to an endless variety of creatures suited to life in or near water. Waterside plants, such as reeds and bulrushes, provide shelter for many of these animals. Wetlands provide important feeding and breeding grounds for many bird species, and act as vital stopover points for water birds migrating across Europe.

In summer, wetlands are alive with insects. Many have two distinct stages in their life cycle, first in water and then in the air. Dragonfly nymphs and mosquito larvae are underwater hunters and scavengers. If they manage to evade predators, they emerge into the air. Other insects are taken by frogs and newts. Both these amphibians, and fish, are prey to birds such as herons, diving mammals like otters and water shrews, and large, sharp-toothed fish such as pike. In many parts of Europe, wetland wildlife is threatened because it is very sensitive to the pollution of water by fertilizers, the pesticides from farmers' fields, and poisonous

waste from factories. Pollution like this is often catastrophic, destroying most or all life in the area. In addition, swamps and bogs are often regarded as wastelands that can be drained and built upon. Western Europe has now lost most of its natural wetlands; those that remain—such as the Camargue in southern France, and Coto Doñana in southwestern Spain—although protected, are still at risk.

### Freshwater hunter

The *pike* is an excellent hunter. It waits motionless in weeds in ambush, then shoots out and grabs its prey. The pike's long jaws are full of sharp teeth—they even grow on the roof of its mouth. The upper teeth are angled backward, so its prey has no chance of escape. Besides other fish, pike will take frogs, water voles, young ducks, and moorhens.

### Brilliant plumage

The *kingfisher* lives by clear, shallow waters that support lots of small fish. It searches for prey from a perch or while hovering above the water. The bird dives almost vertically into the water with its wings stretched back like an arrow, seizes the prey in its beak, then flies off to batter it against a branch before swallowing it whole. Kingfishers nest in burrows dug into the river bank.

## Airy diver

The *water shrew* needs a constant supply of food to keep it warm, so it eats and sleeps in short bursts all day and night. It forages in the water for frogs and fish and on the riverbank for snails, insects, and worms. As it dives, it traps a layer of air in its fur, giving it a silvery appearance. Its large feet are fringed with stiff hairs to help it paddle underwater, and it uses its tail as a rudder. Gripping with its claws, it can walk along the river bed, nosing for food among the rocks and weeds.

## All change

Noisy, water-living *edible frogs* eat insects, crustaceans, and worms. In spring, males gather in ponds and croak to attract females that are full of eggs. A male jumps on a female's back and clutches her until she lays her eggs, then he fertilizes them. The eggs hatch into tadpoles, which have gills like fish. The tadpoles develop arms and legs, lose their tails, and their gills become lungs.

## Born again

Male *dragonflies* establish a territory, and when a female arrives, the male performs a courtship dance. The female lays her eggs on or in the water. The eggs hatch into larvae called nymphs that feed on insects, tadpoles, and small fish. A nymph changes and grows for up to five years. When it is ready for the final change, it climbs up a reed, splits its skin, and the adult dragonfly struggles out. The adult, which feeds in flight on insects such as midges and moths, lives only a month before breeding and dying.

## Stealth and speed

The *heron* wades through water, then waits motionless for a fish to swim by, or it slowly stalks its prey on the riverbank. Then suddenly it strikes, grabbing its victim with its long, pointed beak. It eats fish, frogs, grass snakes, small mammals, and birds, gulping them down alive. Herons nest in large colonies, each pair returning to the same nest year after year. The male defends the nest against rivals and shares incubating and rearing chicks with the female.

## Wetland food chain

Wetland plants provide a food source for many invertebrates, including insects and crustaceans. The plants make their own food using the sun's energy in a process called photosynthesis. Plant-eating invertebrates form a large part of the diet of the edible frog as it hunts in and by the water. The grass snake is active by day, sliding through the wetland vegetation in search of frogs and other prey, which it strikes and swallows whole.

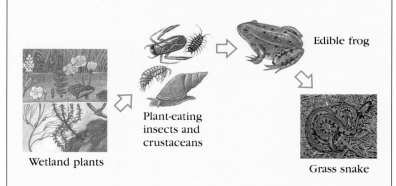

Wetland plants

Plant-eating insects and crustaceans

Edible frog

Grass snake

# THE SOUTH

## EUROPE

Around the northern coast of the Mediterranean Sea, the summers are hot and dry, while the winters are cooler and wetter. The main vegetation consists of scrub. Trees that can withstand dry conditions, such as pines, cedars, and cypresses, provide food and shelter for many creatures, and nest sites for birds. Spring, when the climate is warm and the soil is still moist, is a season of abundance for flowers, flying insects that feed on them, and insect-eating birds.

Many birds will migrate northward to cooler places before the hot summer begins. But some insect-eating birds remain, along with eagles and other birds of prey that swoop on reptiles and rodents, and the lammergeier vulture that soars on high in search of dead sheep or other carrion. Other birds, such as storks, migrate from Africa to nest.

Snakes, lizards, and tortoises sunbathe in the morning to warm themselves, but shelter when the sun gets too hot. Larger mammals, such as the wolf and lynx, are now rare because of the pressure of human populations.

The large numbers of people that visit and live in southern Europe have led to many habitats being destroyed. Land clearance for farming and devastating summer fires have caused further environmental damage. Protected national parks now include the wetlands of the Camargue in southern France and the dunes and forests of Coto Doñana in Spain.

## Sticky feet

The adhesive pads on the *gecko*'s toes enable it to grip and climb up many surfaces, including glass. The pads are covered with millions of microscopic, hairlike structures that act as powerful suckers. Geckoes live among palm fronds, in crevices under tree bark, in rocky outcrops, inside cracks in walls, and around houses. They rest during the day and become active at dusk, hunting by night for insects and spiders.

## Saving the Spanish lynx

This medium-sized, stubby-tailed cat once roamed across all of Spain. The few *lynx* that remain compete with red foxes for rabbits and hares in the sand dunes and pine forests of the Coto Doñana National Park in southwestern Spain. The park itself, which has extensive wetlands that attract storks and flamingoes, is also at risk because its vital ground water is being extracted for agriculture and tourism.

## Cave seals

*Mediterranean monk seals* live in colonies in sea caves in the Mediterranean Sea and the Atlantic Ocean. They are the only seals that live in warm waters. There are now fewer than 500 of them left in the wild. Their numbers have been greatly reduced by fishing and water pollution, and vacationers often disturb the seals when they come ashore onto the beaches to breed. The seal's streamlined body and paddlelike flippers make it a fast and agile swimmer. Its main food is fish and squid.

### Pine processionary moth

○ Spins a flask-shaped nest that hangs from a tree's twigs.
○ At night, a procession of about 100 caterpillars moves nose to tail along branches to find new feeding areas where they can feast on pine needles.
○ Seems vulnerable to predators, but hairs on the caterpillar taste bad, so they are left alone.
○ Considered pests in the pine forests of southern Europe.

### Greater flamingo

○ Feeds with its head down in the water, filtering food with the fine plates inside its bill.
○ Eats protozoa, algae, insects, crustaceans, mollusks, and worms.
○ Pink color comes from carotenoids (natural chemicals found in algae and shrimp).
○ Nests in colonies of thousands, each pair building a mud nest and sharing incubation and rearing of their single chick.

### Hermann's tortoise

○ Likes scrub-covered hillsides and woodlands near the coast.
○ Eats plants and insects.
○ Male courts by biting the female's legs and crashing into her with his shell while squealing like a puppy.
○ Female lays about twelve eggs in a nest scraped in dusty soil.
○ Eggs hatch in about three months.
○ Baby tortoises are independent from birth.

### Fire salamander

○ Hatches from an egg in shallow water as a tadpole. Takes three months to develop fully into an adult.
○ If threatened, secretes (releases) a sticky white poison from glands on its back and behind its head.
○ May have yellow or red markings that warn predators that the salamander is poisonous.
○ Hunts at night for worms, slugs, snails, and insects.

## White beauty

*Camargue horses* live in the wetlands of southern France. They run free, but have owners who ensure their survival and tame some horses, using them to round up wild black bulls. The dominant stallions drive out the young males. Fights between stallions are fierce. Foals are born a year after mating and may suckle for up to two years.

## Good-luck bird

*Storks* pair for life and build a large nest in a tree or on a chimney. They return to the same site each year and mate on the nest. Parents take turns feeding the chicks with regurgitated frogs, insects, lizards, fish, and worms. After about three months, the young learn to fly. At the end of the summer, the storks migrate to southern Africa.

# ASIA

Asia is the largest continent in the world, covering some 17.1 million square miles (44.4m km²). It extends south from the freezing Arctic to the equator, and is separated from Europe in the west by the Ural and Caucasus Mountains, and from North America in the east by the Bering Strait.

While much of Asia consists of rolling plains, a central highland region stretches from west to east. Called the Himalayas, the highest point is over 29,000 feet (8,848 m). In the far north of Siberia, coniferous forests called the taiga have long, bitterly cold winters and are home only to animals that can survive the harsh conditions, like wolves and pine martens. Moving south, the taiga gives way to steppe (open grassland), where many ground-living animals are found. Most of central and southwestern Asia is dry desert, where camels and gerbils have adapted to the hot, dry conditions. The Himalayas separate these barren wastelands from the hot Indian subcontinent and the dense tropical forests of Southeast Asia.

The rapid increase in human population presents a serious threat to many Asian species. The tiger, once widespread throughout Asia, has been reduced to small, isolated populations and may become extinct in the wild. In China, the giant panda, a symbol of animal conservation worldwide, is also facing extinction. Many other smaller and lesser-known species are also endangered.

## Taiga, steppe, and desert

The *marbled polecat* is found all over the steppe and semi-desert. This solitary animal digs a deep burrow with its strong claws. Although it is a good climber, the marbled polecat hunts mainly on the ground, leaving its burrow at dusk to hunt rodents, rabbits, frogs, lizards, snakes, and birds. If threatened, it throws back its head, bares its teeth, and curls its tail over its back to reveal warning markings. Then it squirts an unpleasant scent from glands under its tail. It also uses this scent for marking its territory.

## Mountains

*Musk deer* are shy, solitary animals that live in the forested mountains of central and eastern Asia. No more than 2 feet (60 cm) high, they bound surefootedly across rocks. The male has canine teeth, nearly 3 inches (about 7 cm) long, which it uses to fight other males for a mate. The males also secrete (release) musk from a gland under their belly, which they use to mark their territory. Once hunted for their musk, which is used to make perfume, the deer are now farmed and the musk is taken without killing them.

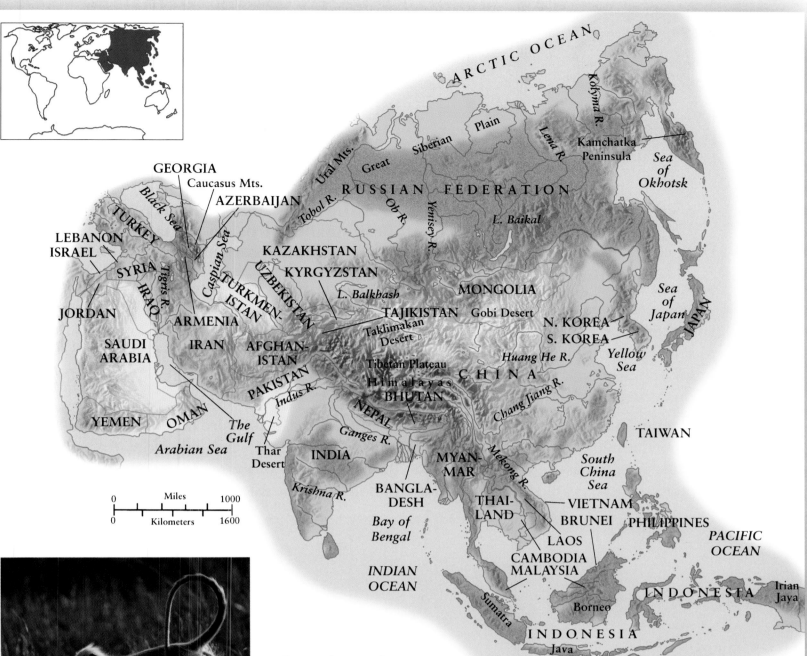

ARCTIC OCEAN

Kolyma R.

Siberian Plain

Kamchatka Peninsula

Sea of Okhotsk

Ural Mts.

Great

RUSSIAN FEDERATION

Tobol R.

Ob R.

Yenisey R.

Lena R.

L. Baikal

GEORGIA

Caucasus Mts.

AZERBAIJAN

Black Sea

TURKEY

KAZAKHSTAN

KYRGYZSTAN

MONGOLIA

Sea of Japan

JAPAN

LEBANON

ISRAEL

SYRIA

Tigris R.

Caspian Sea

TURKMEN-ISTAN

UZBEKISTAN

L. Balkhash

TAJIKISTAN

Gobi Desert

N. KOREA

S. KOREA

Yellow Sea

IRAQ

JORDAN

ARMENIA

IRAN

AFGHAN-ISTAN

Taklimakan Desert

Tibetan Plateau

CHINA

Huang He R.

SAUDI ARABIA

PAKISTAN

Indus R.

Himalayas

BHUTAN

Chang Jiang R.

TAIWAN

YEMEN

OMAN

The Gulf

Arabian Sea

Thar Desert

NEPAL

Ganges R.

INDIA

MYAN-MAR

Mekong R.

South China Sea

PACIFIC OCEAN

Krishna R.

BANGLA-DESH

Bay of Bengal

THAI-LAND

VIETNAM

BRUNEI

PHILIPPINES

INDIAN OCEAN

LAOS

CAMBODIA

MALAYSIA

INDONESIA

Irian Jaya

Sumatra

Borneo

INDONESIA

Java

Miles

0          1000

Kilometers

0          1600

## Indonesia

Some of Indonesia's forest animals have developed a way of gliding from tree to tree to feast on fruits, leaves, and insects that are plentiful all year round. They include the *colugo*, a mammal also known as the "flying lemur." Although it cannot fly like a bird or bat, a membrane called a patagium stretches between its arms, legs, and tail. This gets in the way when the colugo scrambles up a tree trunk, but spread out, it allows the "flying lemur" to glide up to 450 feet (135 m). The young get their first "flying" lessons by clinging to their mother's stomach.

## Tropical forests

*Hanuman langurs* live in groups of up to twenty in the tropical forests of southern Asia. The young are cared for by "aunts," who relieve nursing mothers. A male may try to kill the young when he takes over the group so that the females will breed with him. The females gang together to fight him off, and sometimes they succeed. Moving through the trees or on the ground, langurs eat leaves, flowers, and fruit, sometimes raiding villages for food. People put up with them as they are regarded as sacred; they are named after Hanuman, the Hindu monkey-god.

# TAIGA, STEPPE, AND DESERT

Taiga
Steppe
Desert

The coniferous forest that forms the taiga of northern Asia is the largest forest in the world. The winters are long and harsh, but the short, warm summers see an explosion of life. The trees provide a rich source of food. In late spring, many birds arrive in the forests to feed on the larch, spruce, and fir tree seeds as well as the many insects. Birds of prey, like the goshawk, hunt these smaller birds. In the fall, most birds leave for warmer areas, while many mammals hibernate.

South of the taiga lie the vast steppes of central Asia. Here, the winters are cold and the summers are hot and dry. Spring is the most productive time, when animals start to have young. Smaller ground-dwelling mammals, such as susliks and hamsters, go underground to seek shelter from the cold and from predators, particularly birds of prey. The huge herds of grazing mammals that once roamed the steppe, such as the saiga antelope and European bison, have largely disappeared.

The central Asian deserts lie south of the steppes. Summer days are hot, but temperatures plummet at night, and the winters are often icy cold. Here, animals have to withstand not only drought but also extreme cold. The Bactrian camel, for example, has a long, protective winter coat, and is able to travel for long periods without water.

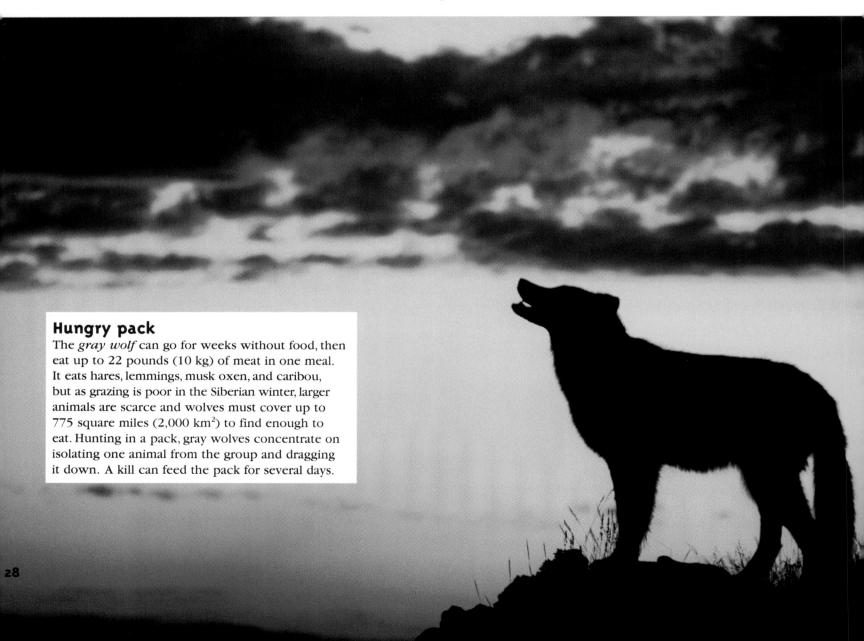

### Hungry pack
The *gray wolf* can go for weeks without food, then eat up to 22 pounds (10 kg) of meat in one meal. It eats hares, lemmings, musk oxen, and caribou, but as grazing is poor in the Siberian winter, larger animals are scarce and wolves must cover up to 775 square miles (2,000 km²) to find enough to eat. Hunting in a pack, gray wolves concentrate on isolating one animal from the group and dragging it down. A kill can feed the pack for several days.

## Suslik

○ Sociable ground squirrel that lives in colonies of many thousands, with burrows sited close together.
○ Changes the steppe vegetation. When burrowing, it brings subsoil to the surface, in which different plants can grow.
○ Droppings fertilize the soil, helping new plants to grow.
○ Hibernates in burrows.

## Pine marten

○ Agile pine-forest dweller.
○ Large paws and sharp claws help it grip branches, and it uses its long, bushy tail for balancing.
○ Catches squirrels and birds in the trees, and rabbits, rodents, and insects on the ground. It also forages for berries.
○ Marks a path through the trees with scent from a gland under its tail.

## Onager

○ Also called wild ass, runs as fast as a racehorse, at around 40 miles per hour (65 km/h).
○ Can survive harsh desert climate for two or three days without drinking.
○ Greatest enemy is humans, but it lives in barren places where few people go.
○ In summer, it eats upland grasses. In winter, the cold and lack of pasture drive it south.

## Mongolian gerbil

○ During the day, the gerbil shelters in its burrow from the intense desert heat.
○ Most active just before sunset, when it comes out in search of grasses and seeds.
○ Never needs to drink and doesn't sweat.
○ Kidneys are adapted to produce small amounts of concentrated urine, so it doesn't waste any water.

## Freshwater seal

Lake Baikal in Russia is the oldest and deepest lake in the world, and three-quarters of its animals are found nowhere else on Earth. The *Baikal seal,* the only seal found in fresh water, probably arrived in the lake when the glaciers melted at the end of the last Ice Age. During the last century, the numbers of Baikal seals were severely reduced by hunting. Recent conservation measures have led to a slight recovery.

## Feather cushion

The male *great bustard* puts on an extraordinary display to attract a mate. He gulps in air to inflate a sac in his throat, which balloons out until his head is thrust back and he seems to turn inside out in a flurry of white feathers. The male mates with four or five females, who incubate the eggs in a shallow scrape nest and rear the chicks alone, feeding them by beak until they learn to peck the grass seeds of the steppe and to eat insects.

29

# HIMALAYAS AND CHINA

The Himalayas form the great mountain system of Asia that separates the cold north from the tropical south. The twin ranges extend over 1,500 miles (2,400 km), from Pakistan across northern India to Bhutan. The highest peaks in the world, including Mount Everest at 29,029 feet (8,848 m), are here. While much of Asia is dry, parts of the Himalayas receive the world's highest rainfall. On the snowcapped peaks, where it is bitterly cold and blizzards are commonplace, nothing can survive. But the crags and valleys at lower altitudes provide a mix of habitats for a wide range of animals.

In the foothills, tropical forests teem with insects, frogs, lizards, snakes, birds, and mammals. Higher up, the tropical trees give way to forests of rhododendrons and bamboo that echo to the musical song of the hill mynah. Above the tree line, grassy meadows are filled with flowers in summer, providing food for butterflies such as the apollo. The snow leopard hunts here for ibex and other prey. Only the yak, with its thick coat, can remain at high altitudes through the coldest months.

The mountains of the east continue into western and central China, covering about one-third of its area. Arctic winds make it bitterly cold in winter, while in summer it is warm and dry. In the misty mountain forests, the giant panda strips bamboo shoots, its only source of food.

## Peaceful giant

*Giant pandas* live alone in the mountain bamboo forests of southwestern China. The bamboo is so low in nutrients that they need to eat for sixteen hours a day. Every fifty years or so, large areas of bamboo flower, seed, and die. Because pandas cannot migrate across farmland or areas of human habitation, sanctuaries are being set up by Chinese conservationists.

## Flashy courtship

The male *golden pheasant* uses his colorful plumage to attract a female during the mating season. He turns the bright feathers around his neck forward to cover his beak like a fan. Golden pheasants build their nests on the ground in the forests of central China. The female incubates the eggs and rears the young alone. The chicks can feed as soon as they hatch, and fly a week later.

## Thick fur

The *snow leopard* lives high in the Himalayas. It preys on sheep, goats, and deer above the tree line in summer. In winter, it follows its prey down to the valleys, where it finds gazelle and wild boar. The hairy pads under its paws help it leap across the snow without sinking. Its beautiful thick pelt is sought after by fur trappers, who have greatly reduced its numbers.

## Brown wings

The *apollo butterfly* sips nectar from the short, hardy plants that bloom in the Himalayas in spring. Its drab colors help it survive the harsh mountain climate—the browns of its wings absorb heat, allowing it to warm up quickly in the sun. Dark colors also shut out the sun's ultraviolet rays (which are stronger in the thin mountain air). Many small mountain creatures have dark coloring for this reason.

## Twisted horns

The *markhor* is a Himalayan goat with corkscrew horns that grow to 4 feet (1.2 m) in the male, and slightly shorter in the female. Hunters have brought the markhor to the edge of extinction. It also catches diseases from the domesticated goats that graze the upland pastures in summer. In the winter, the markhor grows a shaggy coat and moves down the mountain.

## Brilliant mimic

The chattering of the *hill mynah* can be heard in the tropical forests and plantations of the Himalayas and southern China. It lives in small flocks, foraging for fruit and berries, catching insects such as the winged termite, and sipping nectar from flowering trees. Its strong legs and feet are better adapted to perching than to hopping on the ground. In captivity, the hill mynah can mimic human speech accurately.

## Domesticated yaks

*Yaks* are cattle that live on the high Tibetan plain. Their long, shaggy coat protects them from the cold, and they are surefooted enough to cope with the rough terrain. Wild yaks have been hunted almost to extinction, but domesticated yaks are essential for the survival of the mountain people. They provide milk, meat, hides, and wool, and are used as pack animals and to pull carts.

31

# TROPICAL FORESTS

## ASIA

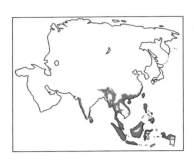

Much of Southeast Asia is covered with a dense green carpet of tropical forest that is warm and wet all year round. About 39 square miles (100 km²) of forest can contain over 400 species of bird, 100 different reptile species, and uncountable species of insect. Tropical forest trees can reach heights of about 100 feet (30 m), and within the forest there are several layers, each with its own characteristic animals.

Above the treetops, insect-eating bats and birds, such as nightjars, dart and swerve to catch flying insects. Below them is the canopy. Birds, such as hornbills, and fruit bats feed on fruit and flowers. Monkeys and squirrels scamper along branches in search of leaves, fruit, and insects, keeping a wary eye out for birds of prey, such as serpent eagles. Gibbons swing gracefully through the branches.

Below this, in the understory, hordes of insects travel up and down the tree trunks and creepers, called lianas. The insects are prey for lizards and tree frogs, both of which are ideal food for tree snakes. Little light gets through to the forest floor, but plenty of food falls from the canopy above for foraging pigs and tapirs. These are prey for large predators, such as tigers, as are the smaller insect-eating mammals.

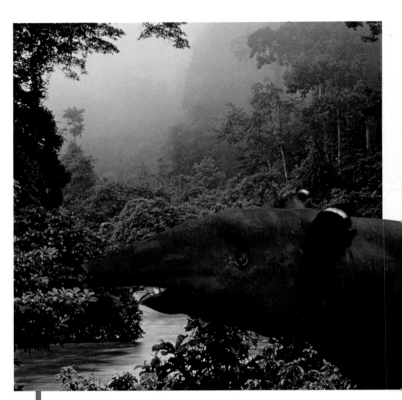

### Flexible snout

A shy, nocturnal (night) creature that scurries along well-worn tracks, the *Malay tapir* lives deep in the tropical forests of Southeast Asia. It uses its long, flexible snout and upper lip like an elephant uses its trunk—to pluck grasses, leaves, buds, and fruit. If surprised by an enemy, the tapir may dive into a swamp to escape. It is a strong swimmer and also eats water plants.

### Toddy cat

A night hunter, the solitary *palm civet* rests in the treetops during the day. It moves stealthily, well camouflaged by its markings, then ambushes its prey. It feeds on small mammals, insects, and fruit and is sometimes called the toddy cat, because it raids palm plantations and steals fermenting palm juice used to make toddy, the local alcoholic drink.

### Is it a leaf?

The *Asian horned frog* is camouflaged to look like the dead leaves that are found on the forest floor. It has three "leaf points," or horns, one over each eye and one above its mouth, and "leaf ribs" on its skin. Its brilliant disguise hides it from predators and prey. The male advertises his presence only in the mating season, when he calls loudly. He risks his life so the female can find him.

## Cock of the roost

The male *red junglefowl* is the ancestor of the domestic rooster, which it looks like. Small groups live at the edge of the rain forest, scratching for roots, seeds, and insects. In spring, the male displays his colorful plumage, then mates with several females. The hens lay their eggs in nests deeply hidden in the undergrowth. Chicks hatch in around three weeks.

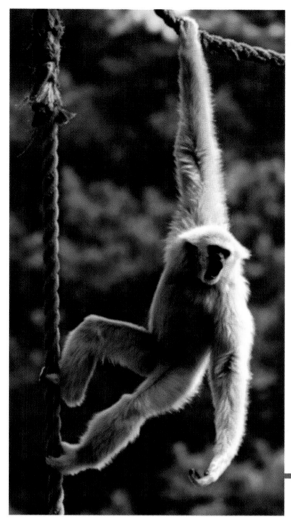

## Swinging ape

The *gibbon*'s long, muscular arms and strong fingers allow it to move by brachiating— swinging arm over arm along the branches. Its shoulder and wrist joints are very mobile, so it can turn right around while hanging by one hand. Gibbons feed on fruit, young leaves, and flowers. At dawn and dusk, they call to each other and to neighboring groups. The female leads a duet with her mate. The baby clings to its mother's fur as she travels, and feeds on her milk for up to two years.

## Project Tiger

In 1900, there were around 40,000 *tigers* in India, but seventy years later, big game hunting and loss of habitat to farmland had reduced the numbers to only 1,800. Project Tiger was set up in 1973. Villagers were rehoused to provide room for tiger sanctuaries. Within ten years, the tiger population had risen to 3,000. Today, work continues to resolve the problem of farmers taking over the tiger's territory and of tigers killing farmers' livestock.

## Snake-eater

The *king cobra* is the largest poisonous snake in the world, over 16 feet (5 m) in length. When aroused, it rears up and spreads the ribs and loose skin at the side of its head to make a hood. Its main prey is other snakes. The female lays a clutch of twenty to forty eggs in a nest of leaves on the forest floor and guards them until they hatch.

**33**

# INDONESIA

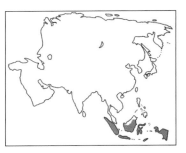

Indonesia, in Southeast Asia, is a massive group of over 13,000 islands, covering about 750,000 square miles (nearly 2m km²) and stretching across 3 million square miles (8m km²) of the Indian Ocean. The main islands include Sumatra, Java, Sulawesi, Kalimantan (part of Borneo), and Irian Jaya (part of New Guinea). Indonesia's islands are mountainous and dotted with volcanoes, some of them active. The climate is tropical with plenty of rain.

Over two-thirds of Indonesia's landscape is covered by tropical forest, and nearly ten percent of the world's rain forests are found here. The forests contain a huge array of animal life. The orangutan feeds on fruit, and Asian elephants and rhinoceroses trundle through the undergrowth, browsing on leaves and branches. Tigers use their striped coats as camouflage to conceal themselves as they stalk unwary prey. A deer darts through the trees, only to be caught by the fearsome Komodo dragon.

Today, uncontrolled logging and the spread of agriculture is tearing the heart out of these forests and threatening many of the animals. As trees disappear, topsoil is washed into the sea, clogging and destroying Indonesia's coral reefs, which are rich in marine life. Indonesia also has vast stretches of mangrove swamps that are rich breeding grounds for fish.

## Long arms

The *orangutan* is a shy, solitary ape. The male, which is much larger than the female, stakes out his territory in the forest and mates with several females, who look after their offspring for about three years. At night, orangutans construct a sleeping platform of branches in the treetops. Their habitat is now under threat and orangutan mothers are often killed and their babies put in zoos.

## Horned nose

The two-horned *Sumatran rhinoceros* uses its prehensile (grasping) upper lip for tearing at shrubs. The young rhinos have a shaggy coat, but lose it as they grow. The adults have little hair to protect them against the sun, so they often wallow in water or mud to cool down. The Sumatran rhino's only enemies are humans and other rhinos—males charge at each other and clash horns.

## Orange horn

Its huge beak allows the *rhinoceros hornbill* to reach fruit growing on the end of slender twigs. The bill is hollow for lightness and strengthened with bony struts. On top of it is a massive "rhinoceros horn" called a casque, which is used for display and to show the bird's status. A strong flier, it lives high in the rain forest canopy and nests in a hole in a tree, plastering over the entrance to leave just a small feeding hole.

## Land-fish

The *mudskipper* lives mostly on land, skipping over the mud in mangrove swamps on its muscular pectoral fins. It breathes by keeping water inside the large cavity around its gills. It shelters in a burrow. Its eyes move independently of one another, searching for crustaceans, insects, and worms. In the mating season, the male develops brighter colors on its back.

## Meat-eating bat

Most bats feed on insects, but the *greater false vampire bat* also preys on small mammals, lizards, frogs, birds, and other bats. It hunts at night, using sight as well as echolocation to find its prey, flying low among trees and undergrowth. The false vampire bites its prey on the back of the neck to kill it, then flies off with it to its roost to feed.

## Slash and burn

Indonesia's tropical forests have come under increasing threat as its population has increased and people need more land to grow crops. As the forests disappear, animals such as the orangutan, found only here, face a difficult future. Forest destruction often takes the form of "slash and burn"— ruthless cutting down of trees and burning vegetation. In the late 1990s, this produced appalling smoke pollution that affected people's health throughout Southeast Asia.

## Huge lizard

At 10 feet (3 m) long, the *Komodo dragon* is the largest land lizard that has ever lived. It can eat a whole deer in one meal, then rest for a week to digest it. Despite their size, Komodo dragons move fast and will eat almost any animal on the hilly forested islands where they live, including other dragons. The males fight to defend their territory and to attract a mate. Baby dragons hatch, fully formed, from large, leathery eggs.

# AFRICA

Africa is the world's second largest continent. In the north are the great wastes of the Sahara Desert, which covers 3.5 million square miles (9m km²)—an area as big as the United States. Here, the addax, desert hedgehog, and sandgrouse survive under the fierce sun. At the steamy heart of Africa, tropical rain forest stretches from the Gulf of Guinea in the west across the Congo Basin. The hot, wet environment produces extremes of size, seen in the tiny royal antelope and the enormous goliath beetle, and richly colored birds, such as the Congo peafowl.

The rain forest gives way to savanna—vast expanses of open grassland dotted with trees and scrubby bushes. The savanna is home to the world's largest herds of grazing animals, as well as the big cats, scavenging dogs, and vultures.

East Africa is dominated by the Great Rift Valley—huge cracks in Earth's crust that have flooded in places to form a chain of long, deep lakes. Crocodiles lurk in the shallows and spectacular flocks of pink flamingoes feed on algae and tiny shrimps. Eagles soar over the mountain ranges, while baboons and the rare ibex leap from crag to crag. In the swamplands that dot the continent, hippos wallow.

## Desert

The *meerkat* is a rabbit-sized animal that lives in the deserts and dry areas of southern Africa. These sociable relatives of the mongoose live in groups and share the work. At daybreak, they warm themselves in the sun while one animal acts as a sentry to watch out for enemies such as eagles. Some babysit the young, and the rest go hunting for lizards, ground-nesting birds, and rodents. Meerkats can kill and eat dangerous prey—they are immune to scorpion and snakebite venom (which would kill a human). At dusk, they take refuge in a network of burrows.

## Savanna

The *impala* is a grass eater that migrates in herds across the savanna. Its markings break up its outline, which confuses predators as the herd swirls and turns to evade them. In the breeding season, the males fight each other for territory in light scrubland that will provide cover for the young. They lock horns in an attempt to throw each other to the ground. (The winner may hold the territory for only a few days until the next rival comes along.) In early summer, when vegetation is at its richest, the females bear a single calf. The young are watched over by their mothers until they are strong enough to run with the herd.

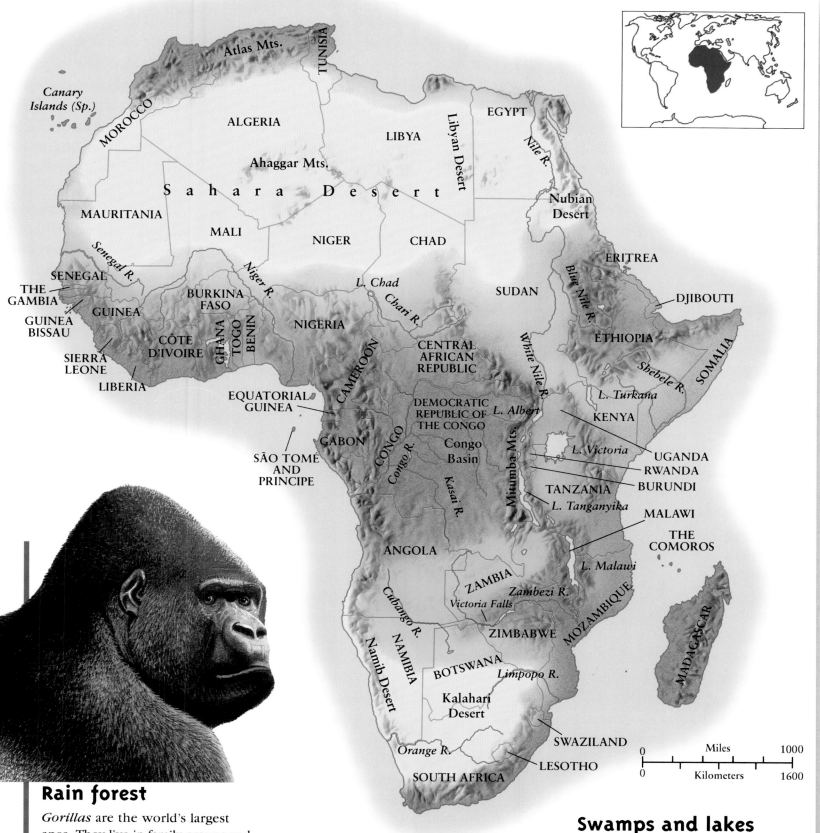

Canary
Islands (Sp.)

Atlas Mts.

TUNISIA

MOROCCO

ALGERIA

LIBYA

EGYPT

Nile R.

MAURITANIA

Ahaggar Mts.

S a h a r a    D e s e r t

Libyan Desert

Nubian
Desert

MALI

NIGER

CHAD

SUDAN

ERITREA

Senegal R.

L. Chad

Blue Nile R.

DJIBOUTI

SENEGAL

THE
GAMBIA

GUINEA
BISSAU

GUINEA

BURKINA
FASO

Niger R.

Chari R.

ETHIOPIA

SIERRA
LEONE

CÔTE
D'IVOIRE

GHANA
TOGO
BENIN

NIGERIA

CENTRAL
AFRICAN
REPUBLIC

White Nile R.

Shebele R.

SOMALIA

LIBERIA

CAMEROON

L. Turkana

EQUATORIAL
GUINEA

DEMOCRATIC
REPUBLIC OF
THE CONGO

L. Albert

KENYA

SÃO TOMÉ
AND
PRINCIPE

GABON

CONGO

Congo R.

Congo
Basin

Kasai R.

Mitumba Mts.

L. Victoria

UGANDA
RWANDA
BURUNDI

TANZANIA

L. Tanganyika

MALAWI

THE
COMOROS

ANGOLA

L. Malawi

ZAMBIA

Zambezi R.

Victoria Falls

MOZAMBIQUE

MADAGASCAR

Cubango R.

ZIMBABWE

Namib Desert

NAMIBIA

BOTSWANA

Limpopo R.

Kalahari
Desert

SWAZILAND

Orange R.

LESOTHO

SOUTH AFRICA

| 0 | Miles | 1000 |
| 0 | Kilometers | 1600 |

## Rain forest

*Gorillas* are the world's largest
apes. They live in family groups and
feed on leaves, shoots, and stems.
A mature male, known as a silverback
because of the color of his hair, leads
the group. Up to sixteen years old,
weighing around 440 pounds
(200 kg), silverbacks are too heavy
to be tree-dwellers. The females and
their young may climb into the trees
to feed and sleep. If challenged by a
young male, a silverback will roar and
beat his chest, but gorillas are rarely
aggressive. Because of hunting and
the destruction of their forest habitat,
fewer than 1,000 gorillas remain.

## Swamps and lakes

The *Nile crocodile* was once found
all over Africa. It preys on wildebeest,
gazelle, buffalo, and lions, and will
also eat people. The crocodile
ambushes its prey, then drags it
underwater to drown it. It stores the
dead creature underwater until it
begins to rot. The crocodile cannot
chew, but tears off huge chunks of
flesh and gulps them down. It eats
every scrap, digesting everything
with stones it has swallowed to
grind the food in its stomach.

37

# SAVANNA

## AFRICA

The African savanna is one of the last great natural grasslands on Earth. It is home to many of the world's largest land mammals, both plant eaters (herbivores) and their predators (carnivores). The grasses are heavily cropped by large herds of herbivores such as zebras and gazelles. New shoots appear as taller stalks are nibbled off. Each species feeds on a different part of the grass, so they do not compete with one another. Other herbivores are browsers: Rhinos eat scrubby twigs, while elephants and giraffes pluck leaves from tall trees.

Many grazers and browsers are the food of lions, leopards, and wild dogs. After the killers have feasted, vultures and other scavengers, such as hyenas, move in. Within hours, the bones are picked bare, and carrion flies and beetles can finish the job.

The savanna has two seasons, hot and wet and hot and dry. As the grasses become parched, the herds move to fresh grazing lands. When the warm rains come, the land turns green. Within a few days during the wet season, all the females of a grazing herd give birth. This means that, although their predators have a feast, as many young as possible survive.

### Striped horse

For most of the year, *zebras* live in scattered groups of ten to fifteen animals, usually one male and the rest females and their foals. In the dry season, they mass into large herds that stretch as far as the eye can see. There is safety in numbers, but as zebras gallop across the savanna, some fall prey to predators such as lions, wild dogs, and hyenas.

### Tender mother

The *scorpion* hunts at night by detecting the vibrations of its prey. It grabs its victim with its pincers, sometimes using its sting to paralyze it. The sting of some scorpions can kill large animals and people. A scorpion lays about 100 eggs. When they hatch, the young climb onto their mother's back until they are able to fend for themselves.

### Endangered rhino

The *black rhino* has been hunted to the verge of extinction for its nose horn, which poachers sell to be carved into dagger handles and crushed to make traditional medicines. Some people still believe it has mysterious powers, but rhino horn is actually made of keratin, the same material that forms human hair and nails. Some conservationists have tried to save black rhinos by sawing off their horns before they fall victim to poachers. This is a painless process for the rhinos.

## Ostrich

- World's largest bird.
- Can't fly but can run faster than any other animal on two legs, sprinting up to 43 miles per hour (70 km/h).
- Only bird in the world with just two toes on its foot. It has very sharp claws and can give a deadly kick in self-defense.
- Lays the largest eggs, twenty times as big as a hen's egg.
- Males and females pair up to breed, sharing nest duty. But other females also lay in the nest, so the birds sit on up to forty eggs.

## African hunting dog

- Also called the African wild dog, lives in packs of between six and twenty animals.
- Rests during the day and hunts at dawn and dusk.
- Prey includes zebra and impala. Returns to the den to disgorge food for the dogs that stayed behind with the young.
- Very social animals, sharing care for the young, old, and sick in the pack.
- Nomadic, settling down for three months of the year, when the pups are born in an underground den.

## Wildebeest

- Herds roam thousands of miles across the savanna in search of grass.
- When they graze, they protect their young by surrounding them.
- Give birth standing up. The baby gets to its feet immediately and can run with the herd in a few hours.
- Herds of wildebeest and zebra often merge to provide greater protection against prowling predators like lions.

## Secretary bird

- A bird of prey that does not swoop but stomps on its prey to kill it, then tears it apart using its beak.
- Can be 4 feet (1.2 m) tall, wings can span 6 ½ feet (2 m).
- Soars in the air like other birds of prey, but spends most of its time walking.
- Pairs for life, sleeping with its mate in their nest all year round.
- Feeds on rodents, insects, and snakes, regurgitating its prey for its young.

## Top cat

*Lions* live in a pride of twenty to thirty animals. Each pride has up to four males, distinguished by their manes. Male cubs are driven from the pride at two years old. Rival lions often fight to the death. The lionesses do most of the work, sharing cub-care and hunting in an organized group while the males rest. When they kill an animal, they may wait until the male has eaten before feeding themselves.

## Intelligent giant

*African elephants* are the world's largest land animals. Calves are suckled by their mother for two years, then, between the ages of eight and twenty, the young bulls are driven from the herd and form a separate bachelor group. An elephant rips leaves from the trees with its trunk and tusks and uses its trunk, an extension of its upper lip and nose, as a "hand" to feed itself.

39

# TROPICAL RAIN FOREST

## AFRICA

The African rain forest stretches from the west coast to the Rift Valley. Wildlife thrives in this permanently warm, humid, evergreen environment. Tall emergent trees push through the forest canopy. In clearings where a tree has fallen, saplings thrust up toward the light. Monkeys swing through the trees and crowned eagles soar, looking for birds and squirrels. Pythons coil around branches, chimps and gorillas eat leaves and fruit, and butterflies flit through the air. Antelopes browse on bushes; wild pigs, porcupines, and termites eat leaves and rotting fruit; and pygmy hippos bathe in swamps.

There is plenty to eat in the tropical rain forests and some species grow extra large. The African giant snail is the biggest in the world—its shell is 10 inches (25 cm) across, almost the size of a soccer ball. The goliath frog swallows mice whole and the praying mantis can kill small lizards. Camouflage is important in the densely populated forest. Predators such as leopards are difficult to spot in dappled shade. The splashy markings on genets (catlike hunters) and antelopes make them almost invisible as rays of light fall on the dark undergrowth. There are green tree snakes and some moths that look like leaves.

### Chatterbox

The *gray parrot* screeches and whistles in the rain forest, where it feeds on seeds, nuts, and fruit. It roosts in the treetops at night and makes a nest in a tree hole in the breeding season. Two of the parrot's toes point forward and two backward, which makes it easy for it to clamber in trees, using its hooked beak as a "third foot." It also uses its foot to grip food. Because it is a good mimic and can be taught to "talk," the gray parrot is at risk from poachers, who sell birds to the pet trade.

### Armor-plated

The *pangolin* lives in the trees and moves from branch to branch, grasping the bark with its feet and its prehensile tail, which grips like an extra foot. Its skin is covered with scales that overlap and help to protect it from predators. When attacked, it rolls into a ball, safe from all but hyenas and the largest cats. The pangolin eats termites and ants. It uses its claws to rip into a nest, sweeping them up with flicks of its long tongue.

### Spotted hunter

The *leopard* is a solitary member of the cat family that marks its territory with claw marks and urine. It often hunts near water, waiting in a tree for its prey to come to drink. It eats fish, birds, snakes, monkeys, okapi, and antelope, dragging its kill into a tree, where scavengers can't steal it. This provides the leopard with food for several days.

## Hungry bride

The *praying mantis* gets its name from the way it waits, motionless, as if in prayer. It turns its head as it waits for an insect to come into range, then shoots out its arms to grab it. The mantis scoops out the juicy bits of its prey with its mouthparts, leaving the tough shell, wings, and legs. The female is larger than the male and often eats her partner while they are mating.

## Clever chimp

*Chimpanzees* live in troops of fifteen to eighty animals. They eat fruit, leaves, insects, grubs, and honey. Sometimes they kill larger animals, such as monkeys. At night, chimps sleep in a nest they make in the trees. The young travel on their mother's back. They are weaned at about four years old, but remain dependent for several more years. The chimp is a highly intelligent animal and can use sticks as tools.

## Deadly fangs

The poisonous *gaboon viper* can be 6 ½ feet (2 m) long. Its fangs are the longest of any snake—up to 2 inches (5 cm)—and one bite could kill a human. It hides on the forest floor, where its markings in buff, purple, pink, and brown provide excellent camouflage among the leaf litter. It eats frogs, birds, and rodents. It can give birth to sixty live young, which are able to fend for themselves as soon as they are born.

## Honey lovers

The *ratel*, also known as the honey badger, often teams up with a bird called a *honeyguide*. To attract the ratel's attention, the honeyguide flicks its tail and makes a loud chattering noise. Then the bird leads the ratel to a bees' nest. The ratel breaks open the nest with its claws as the bird looks on, then both creatures eat the honey and grubs inside.

# DESERTS

## AFRICA

The Sahara is the largest desert on Earth. The scorching sun beats down by day, but at night it gets extremely cold and it hardly ever rains. One-tenth of the Sahara is made up of sand dunes; the rest is rock, silt, and gravel. But few parts of the desert are completely barren. Tough grasses and spiny bushes grow in the stony wastelands. Other plants have fleshy leaves and stalks that absorb the heavy dew. When rain falls, seeds sprout after lying dormant for months or years, and the desert floor is carpeted briefly with flowers.

The creatures that live in the Sahara and Africa's southern deserts, the Kalahari and the Namib, have adapted to survive harsh conditions. Insects, scorpions, and spiders have a hard, shiny skin to stop their bodies from drying out. Reptiles such as snakes and lizards need the sun's warmth to make them active. Some animals, like the sand cat, have thick fur under their feet to protect them against the burning ground. The lack of water is the greatest challenge to survival. Many animals, like the barbary sheep, get all the moisture they need from eating plants. Desert mammals hardly sweat at all, and their urine is concentrated, so they do not lose excess water.

## High jump

The *desert jerboa* is a small rodent like a tiny kangaroo. Its strong back legs are four times as long as its front legs, and it can jump more than 8 feet (about 2.5 m) to escape from its predators. Its long tail helps it to balance. The jerboa uses its short arms for burrowing in the desert sand. During the day, it rests in its burrow, coming out at dusk to eat insects and seeds. Plants provide all the moisture the jerboa needs, so it never has to drink.

## Tiny fox

The *fennec fox* is the smallest of the foxes, and grows to only 16 inches (40 cm). Its huge ears, 6 inches (15 cm) long, act like a radiator to give off heat and help the animal keep cool. They also provide the fennec fox with excellent hearing. It hunts mainly by sound, listening out for termites and other insects, lizards, and jerboas. By day, it rests and shelters from the fierce heat in its burrow.

## Snakes and ladders

The *desert horned viper* moves across the loose sand in an unusual way, leaving telltale "ladder" tracks. It burrows by wriggling until it has disappeared into the sand, leaving only its eyes and nostrils peeping out to watch for prey or danger. It hunts mainly at night, feeding on small creatures such as lizards.

## Spiny tail

Reptiles control their body temperature by gaining or losing heat from the environment. They need less energy and food than warm-blooded creatures, which have to generate heat in their own body. The *dabb spiny-tailed lizard* stores fat in its spiny tail. It can live on this if it finds no insects or plants to eat. It also uses the spines on its tail to defend itself against enemies.

## Rare survivor

The *addax* can survive extreme heat and drought. Its wide hooves stop it from sinking into the sand as it searches for the scant desert vegetation. It gets all its moisture from grasses and leaves and never needs to drink. A shy creature, it has been hunted (for its skin and meat) and is now very rare.

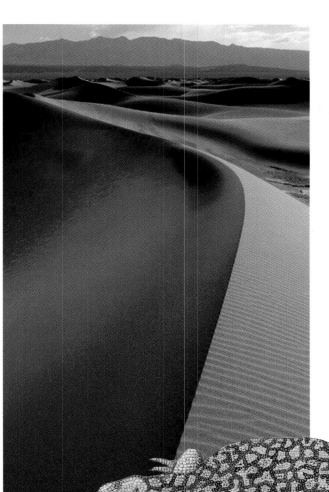

## Desert cleaner

*Dung beetles* clean up the desert by eating the droppings of other animals. They roll the dung into marble-sized balls, then trundle them to their nests, pushing the balls along with their back legs. At their nesting site, they bury the dung balls, first laying an egg in each one. In this way, the hatching beetles are provided with a good supply of nutritious food.

## Ship of the desert

The *dromedary*, or Arabian camel, has a single hump. This is made up mainly of fat, to keep the camel going. The camel can survive for weeks without food or drink, but when it gets to water, it will gulp nearly 55 quarts (50 l) in a few minutes. In sandstorms, its long, thick eyelashes protect its eyes, and it can close its nostrils. Camels can travel up to 30 miles (50 km) a day. Their swaying walk has earned them the affectionate nickname "ship of the desert."

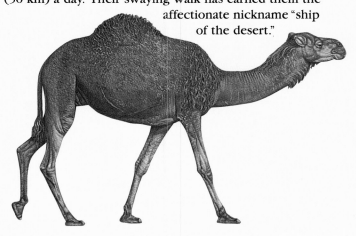

# WETLANDS AND MOUNTAINS

## AFRICA

Africa's wetlands include the great lakes of the eastern Rift Valley, the swamps and floodplains of the Okavango delta in Botswana, and the Kafue floodplain in Zambia. Wetlands are packed with animal life as well as fish like the Nile perch. Wetland antelopes, such as the lechwe, feed on the lush vegetation and seek refuge in the water if a predator appears. Hippos need water to shelter them from the fierce sun during the day. Water birds feed in the wetlands, and many stop there while migrating. Crocodiles lurk in the swamps, ready to snap up passing prey.

To the east of equatorial Africa lie several mountain ranges. The single highest peak, at almost 20,000 feet (6,000 m), is Mount Kilimanjaro. These mountains are tropical and are exposed to hot, intense sunshine during the day and freezing cold nights. The mountains are rich in animal life, which changes with increasing altitude. At the lowest level is savanna grassland. Higher up are montane forests of cedar and camphor trees and, higher still, bamboo forests. The forests and clearings are home to many birds, such as parrots, and large mammals, including black rhinos and elephants, primates such as bushbabies, and predators such as lions. Few large animals venture above the tree line to the high alpine meadows and heathlands. Here rodents and hyraxes live, always watchful of danger from eagles. Unusual alpine plants grow here, like the giant lobelia that provides food for the scarlet tufted malachite sunbird. At the top, the bare rock and snow provide no shelter for wildlife.

## WETLANDS
### Daytime wallowers

The heavyweight *hippopotamus* wallows in the muddy waters of lakes and rivers to cool off in the heat of the day and avoid burning its hairless skin. Being in water in a herd provides extra protection for young hippos from enemies. Male hippos compete for mates by opening their mouth wide to show off their massive tusks. Despite their large size, hippos are excellent swimmers and divers. At night, they leave the water and follow well-worn paths to "hippo meadows" where they graze on grasses until dawn.

### Swimming antelope

The *lechwe* is an antelope that lives in lake and riverside marshes. Lechwes are sociable animals that wade in the water, grazing on water plants and grass. If threatened by a cheetah or lion, they quickly leap through the water. They are good swimmers, and can go underwater with just their nostrils showing. Lechwes only go onto dry land to rest and give birth.

### Lily trotter

The long-toed spreading feet of the *African jacana* allow it to walk over lily pads and other water plants without sinking, giving it its other name, the lily trotter. The jacana feeds on insects and crustaceans. If threatened, it hides underwater with only its bill and nostrils showing. The male makes a floating nest for his mate, and he incubates the eggs and rears the chicks himself.

# MOUNTAINS
## Sun-lovers

The sociable, rabbit-sized *rock hyrax* makes its home in caves on rocky outcrops, where up to 100 live together, emerging in the morning to warm up in the sun. They survive on very little water and crop plants with their cheek teeth. They bare their long incisors (front teeth) in self-defense. Their feet have rubbery soles, which give a good grip for climbing.

## Rare feast

The long-beaked *scarlet-tufted malachite sunbird* sips nectar from lobelia flowers. As it feeds, it gets brushed with pollen and this fertilizes the next lobelia it visits. Unlike a hummingbird, it perches instead of hovers and it eats insects. To attract a female, the male displays his red tuft and shivers his wings. The pair build a nest stuck together with spiders' webs.

## Big hair

The *gelada* is a baboon that lives in the mountains. The male has a thick mane hanging down his back. The bare patch of red skin on his chest expands when he is frightened or angry. Each male heads a group of about twelve females and their young. During the day, geladas descend to the grasslands to feed, returning higher up the mountain at dusk to sleep on a rocky ledge.

## Feet first

Soaring on updrafts of warm air, *Verreaux's eagle* scours the mountains with its sharp eyes for rabbits and rock hyraxes. Then it swoops down, kills its prey with a heavy blow from its foot, and grips it in its talons. In the breeding season, Verreaux's eagles take their catch to the nest to feed to their young. They also feed on the carcasses of animals that have slipped and fallen to their death.

## Upsetting the balance

Lake Victoria in East Africa was once home to 300 species of *cichlid* fish. Cichlids are unusual in that they brood their young in their mouth. In the 1960s, Nile perch were introduced into the lake as a catch for fishermen. The perch fed on the cichlids and multiplied rapidly, providing local people with plenty to eat. But the cichlids declined, and now at least 200 of the species are extinct.

# NORTH AMERICA

North America is the world's third largest continent with an area of some 926,000 square miles (24.4m km²) and a huge range of habitats. Despite the destruction of some of the continent's wild places for industrial development, building, and agriculture, these habitats still contain a vast variety of animal life. North America stretches from the cold polar regions of northern Canada in the north, to the tropical forests of Central America in the south, and is bordered by the mighty Pacific Ocean in the west and the Atlantic in the east.

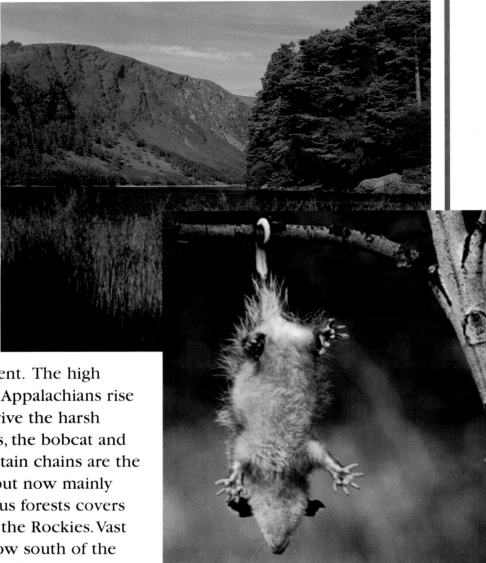

Two mountain chains dominate the continent. The high Rockies run down the west side, while the Appalachians rise in the east. Hardy sheep and goats can survive the harsh mountain conditions, as can their predators, the bobcat and lynx. Stretched out between the two mountain chains are the fertile Great Plains, once prairie grassland but now mainly agricultural land. A broad band of coniferous forests covers much of the north, as well as the slopes of the Rockies. Vast broad-leaved forests of maples and oaks grow south of the Great Lakes and on both sides of the Appalachians. In spring and summer, these are filled with insects, birds, and mammals. Warm wetlands in the southeast form an ideal habitat for water birds and alligators. By contrast, the southwest is a dry area of deserts, where many animals seek shade during the day and emerge to feed at night.

## Forests

The *Virginia opossum* is North America's only marsupial. Like the kangaroo, it has a pouch on its belly into which the tiny, underdeveloped young are born. The cat-sized opossum has a litter of up to twenty young, but only the strongest survive, as the mother does not have enough nipples in her pouch to feed them all. It nests on the ground and forages in leaf litter on the forest floor and in trees for its food, such as insects, fruit, and small mammals. It is a good climber with strong claws for gripping and a prehensile tail, which it twines around branches to serve as a fifth limb.

## Mountains

The *mountain bluebird* is a kind of thrush. It is found in open meadowland dotted with trees high in the Rockies. The male has beautiful blue plumage, while the female is a duller gray-brown. They make their nest in a tree hole and rear about five chicks. In summer, the mountain bluebird lives above 5,000 feet (1,500 m), feeding on insects caught on the wing. In winter, bluebirds move down the mountains and gather in flocks to feed on fruit. Some migrate south to Mexico.

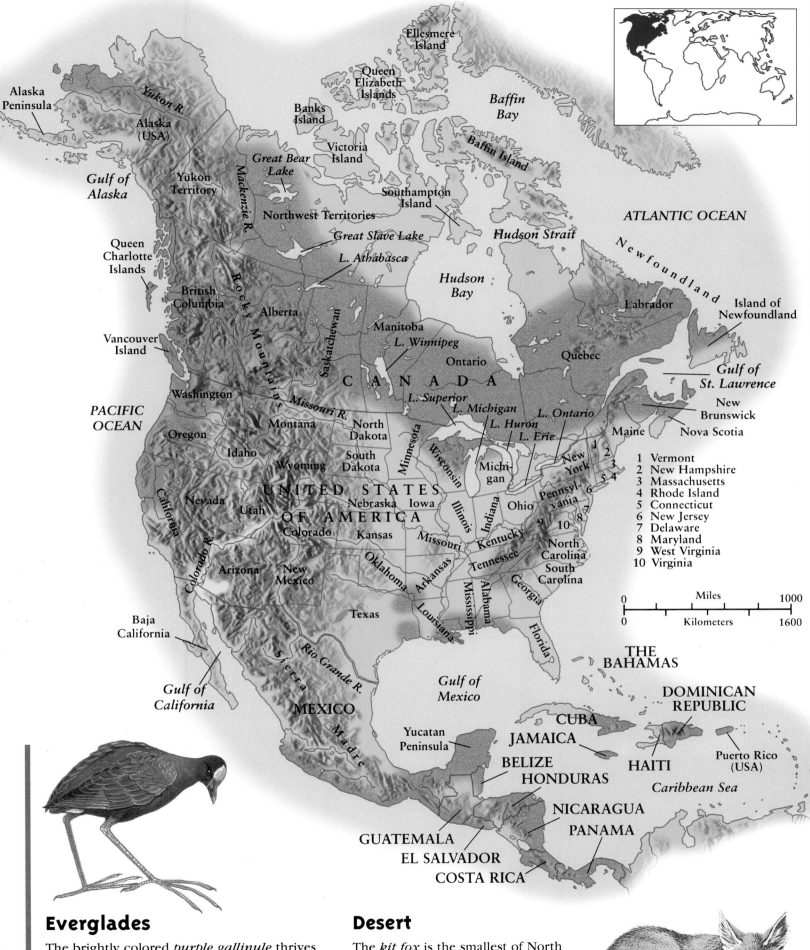

Alaska Peninsula
*Yukon R.*
Alaska (USA)
*Gulf of Alaska*
Yukon Territory
*Mackenzie R.*
Northwest Territories
Great Bear Lake
Banks Island
Victoria Island
Queen Elizabeth Islands
Ellesmere Island
*Baffin Bay*
*Baffin Island*
Great Slave Lake
L. Athabasca
Southampton Island
*Hudson Strait*
ATLANTIC OCEAN
*Newfoundland*
Queen Charlotte Islands
British Columbia
Alberta
Saskatchewan
Manitoba
*Hudson Bay*
Labrador
Island of Newfoundland
*Rocky Mountains*
L. Winnipeg
Ontario
Quebec
*Gulf of St. Lawrence*
Vancouver Island
C A N A D A
PACIFIC OCEAN
Washington
*Missouri R.*
Montana
North Dakota
*L. Superior*
L. Michigan
L. Huron
L. Ontario
L. Erie
New Brunswick
Nova Scotia
Maine
Oregon
Idaho
Wyoming
South Dakota
*Minnesota*
*Wisconsin*
Michigan
New York
*California*
Nevada
Utah
UNITED STATES
Nebraska
Iowa
*Illinois*
*Indiana*
Ohio
Pennsylvania
Colorado
*Colorado R.*
OF AMERICA
Kansas
Missouri
Kentucky
West Virginia
North Carolina
Arizona
New Mexico
Oklahoma
Arkansas
Tennessee
Mississippi
Alabama
Georgia
South Carolina
Baja California
*Rio Grande R.*
Texas
Louisiana
*Florida*
*Sierra Madre*
*Gulf of California*
MEXICO
*Gulf of Mexico*
Yucatan Peninsula
THE BAHAMAS
CUBA
JAMAICA
BELIZE
HONDURAS
GUATEMALA
EL SALVADOR
COSTA RICA
NICARAGUA
PANAMA
HAITI
DOMINICAN REPUBLIC
Puerto Rico (USA)
*Caribbean Sea*

1 Vermont
2 New Hampshire
3 Massachusetts
4 Rhode Island
5 Connecticut
6 New Jersey
7 Delaware
8 Maryland
9 West Virginia
10 Virginia

| 0 | Miles | 1000 |
|---|---|---|
| 0 | Kilometers | 1600 |

# Everglades

The brightly colored *purple gallinule* thrives in the lush, warm swamplands of the Florida Everglades. Its long, spreading toes allow it to walk easily over lily pads and other floating plants, searching for small fish, frogs, and water insects. It is also an agile climber. It hops up reeds and rice plants to eat the seeds, and feeds on berries in bushes. It builds a cup-shaped nest close to the water.

# Desert

The *kit fox* is the smallest of North America's foxes and lives in the arid wastelands of the western deserts. It hunts at night, using its large ears and good hearing to locate lizards, rodents, and rabbits. It approaches stealthily, then leaps in the air and lands on its prey, squashing it with its front paws. Solitary for most of the year, the foxes share the job of parenting. Cubs are born in a den, and both parents bring them food once they are weaned.

# FORESTS AND WOODLANDS

## NORTH AMERICA

Coniferous forests of spruce, pine, larch, and fir stretch for almost 4,000 miles (6,400 km), from Alaska and across most of Canada, broken only by lakes and rivers. Here, the summers are warm, but the winters are bitterly cold. The lynx and its main prey, the snowshoe hare, have thickly furred feet to stop them from sinking into deep snow. The short summer sees the arrival of insect-eating birds to breed, and the departure of the caribou (reindeer) to the colder, treeless tundra farther north. Birds of prey feed on rodents that are plentiful in summer.

Forests
Woodlands

The woodlands south of the Great Lakes and on both sides of the Appalachian Mountains in Canada and the United States are filled with over 150 species of deciduous, broad-leaved trees, including maple, oak, and beech. These provide a rich habitat for many animals. As the spring sunlight warms the forest floor, wild flowers spring up and the trees start to regain their leaves. The flowers provide food for insects and rodents. Many birds—both new arrivals from winter homes and year-round residents—feed on insects as they build their nests and breed. Hawks and owls, as well as raccoons and opossums thrive. In the fall, the leaves turn red and gold before they drop.

### Champion migrant

In the fall, millions of *monarch butterflies* set off from Canada and the northern United States on a huge migration to California and Mexico. Here, they hibernate in winter roosting sites, completely covering the trees. In spring, they awake and flutter to the ground to sip nectar from milkweed flowers. Then they begin flying north. During the journey, many mate, lay eggs on milkweed leaves, then die. The eggs hatch into caterpillars, which soon develop into butterflies, which continue their parents' flight north.

### Watery feast

In the winter, *moose* browse on trees and bushes in forests across the far north of North America, Canada, and Alaska. In summer, their main diet is water plants—they often wade up to their shoulders in marshy lakes to feed. Moose stand up to 7 ½ feet (2.3 m) tall at the shoulder and need about 45 pounds (20 kg) of vegetation a day to keep them going. In the harsh winter, many die of starvation or get stranded in deep snow and fall prey to wolves.

48

## Singing frog

Living in damp woodland habitats in the eastern United States, the *spring peeper* is a tree frog less than an inch (about 2 cm) long. Sticky pads on its long, thin fingers and toes give a good grip while it climbs trees in search of insect prey. In spring, the male fills a sac in his throat with air, then "peeps" or chirps to attract a mate. A chorus of thousands of peepers is an early sign of spring.

## Ear ear

Owls have acute hearing and large, very light-sensitive eyes. They fly silently with down-covered flight feathers that muffle the air passing through them. With its wailing call, the *eastern screech owl* roosts in a hole in a tree and hunts at night for insects, birds, and squirrels. Its ear tufts express its mood: Raised when the owl is excited and flattened when it is at rest.

## Knock on wood

A rapid drumming noise often signals the presence of a *pileated woodpecker*. This long-bodied bird with short legs has a distinctive red crest. It grips the bark of a tree with its strong claws, supports its body with its tail, and drills into dead wood for insects such as the carpenter ant. The spongy bone at the base of the woodpecker's beak acts as a cushion against the hammering.

## Prickly customer

Long toe claws and an excellent sense of balance help the *North American porcupine* climb trees in search of new shoots and fruit. By night, it sleeps in a hollow tree. If attacked, it erects its spines and lashes its barbed tail from side to side. The loosely attached spines stick into the predator's flesh and slowly work their way in deeper. However, enemies such as bobcats and wolverines are skilled at flipping porcupines over and attacking their soft underbelly.

## Landscape artist

The industry of the *beaver* controls floods, slows erosion, and creates new wetlands. With their huge incisor teeth, beavers fell trees, which they nudge and float into position across fast-flowing streams. Then they build dams with sticks, stones, and mud. The area behind the dam is flooded, creating a large pool. The beaver builds a nest called a lodge, with an underwater entrance, in the middle of the pool. Here, the beaver family can shelter from predators and cold weather.

49

# MOUNTAINS

## NORTH AMERICA

Two huge mountain ranges—the Rockies and Appalachians—run north to south on opposite sides of North America. In the west, the Rocky Mountains stretch for 3,200 miles (5,150 km), from Alaska to Mexico. They include over 700 mountains of over 10,000 feet (3,050 m)—the highest peak, at 20,321 feet (6,194 m), is in Alaska. The higher you go, the colder and wetter it becomes. At the lowest levels, mixed forests are home to white-tailed deer, porcupines, and red foxes. In the higher coniferous forests, black bears forage for roots and berries, while predatory cougars and wolves roam. Above the treeline, summer alpine meadows are rich in insects that provide food for mountain bluebirds. Surefooted mountain goats and bighorn sheep descend from rocky crags to graze with pikas and marmots. The Rockies and its national parks provide a refuge for animals that have been lost from other parts of North America.

In the east, the Appalachians stretch for about 1,500 miles (2,400 km), from Quebec in Canada to Alabama in the United States. The Appalachians do not reach above 6,700 feet (2,050 m), but their northern areas experience some of the worst winter weather on Earth. The Appalachians have the same life zones as the Rockies, although the warmer southern peaks do not rise above the treeline. Here, animals such as white-tailed deer and spotted skunks are found on both upper and lower slopes.

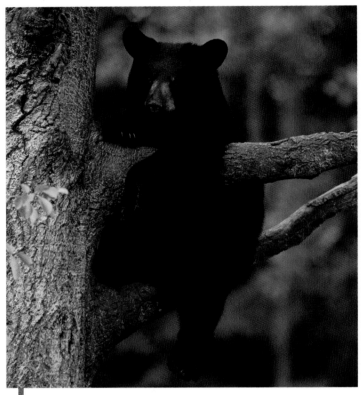

## Winter sleep

The *American black bear* eats plants, insects, and fruits, but it will also take grubs, rodents, carrion, and fish. Its sharp claws are used for digging, tearing food, and climbing trees. It goes into a winter sleep in a tree hollow lined with dry plants. Born blind and naked in January, the cubs are suckled until they are ready to leave the den and learn to forage for themselves.

## Headbanging

In the rutting season, male *bighorn sheep* charge and butt heads, reeling back dizzily after the collision. Sometimes they tussle with their long, curling horns in a desperate battle for territory and a mate. The horns of the female are much shorter. Bighorns are agile climbers and can leap nimbly from crag to crag. Their cloven (divided) hooves separate into two halves to help them grip the rocks.

## White signal flag

The *white-tailed deer* is widespread in mountains and forests. It uses its short white tail as an alarm signal for other deer. At the approach of danger, it flicks its tail up and down, and the small herd instantly darts away. The white tails may also help the deer follow each other. In summer, white-tailed deer eat grasses, fruits, nuts, and blossoms. In winter, they use strong cheek teeth to browse on twigs.

## Scaling the peaks

Herds of *North American mountain goats* live in the snowfields and near the glaciers of the Rockies. In the snow, they are camouflaged from predators like wolves and cougars by their warm, white coats. Their curved toes help them cling to steep, slippery slopes. When the kids are born, they scramble to their feet and in a few days are ready to leap across the rocks with the herd.

## Grass harvest

*Pikas* live singly or in pairs among the rocks in remote mountainous areas. They make a nest in a crack or crevice. In summer and fall, they eat grasses, shoots, and flowers while collecting stores of food for the winter. They call out to defend their territory from intruders, but dart for cover among the rocks if threatened.

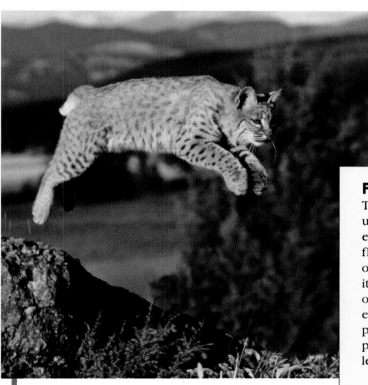

## Food chain

The *northern goshawk* hunts in upland meadows and at the forest edge. It either maneuvers in low flight through the trees or waits on a perch and swoops down on its victim. It preys mainly on other birds in flight, but also eats small mammals, such as pikas. Pikas, in turn, live off juicy plant material, including grass, leaves, and new shoots.

## Scent signals

The *bobcat* marks its territory with scrapes, urine, and droppings. By sniffing a female's urine, a male knows when she is ready to mate. Her droppings tell other females if she has kittens. Mother bobcats are very aggressive when defending their young. Bobcats hunt at night for rabbits and hares, creeping up silently until close enough to pounce, then killing them with a bite to the base of the neck.

# PRAIRIE

## NORTH AMERICA

The word prairie comes from the French for "large meadow," but the North American prairies are more than large. They range from the Great Lakes in the east to the Rockies in the west, and from the dry Mexican plateau to the Canadian forests, covering 568,000 square miles (1.47m km$^2$). They are bitterly cold in winter and baking hot in summer. They were once just grasslands as there was not enough rain for trees to grow. As Europeans settled in North America in the 19th century, the prairies were turned over for agriculture.

The prairie soil, among the richest in the world, was used to grow wheat, corn, and other grain. Other areas were grazed by cattle and sheep, pushing out the native prairie species. The large grassland mammals, the bison and the antelopelike pronghorn, were almost wiped out by farming. Today, intensive agriculture has left few areas of natural prairie, although efforts are being made to restore it by planting native grasses. In natural prairie, ground-dwellers are the most common animals in the treeless landscape. Ground squirrels, such as prairie dogs, live in extensive burrows, where they hibernate through the winter. While feeding on grasses, they may be taken by birds of prey such as the red-tailed hawk, by burrowing owls, or by a coyote. This dog relative eats a wide variety of prey that also includes ground-living birds such as the sage grouse and the prairie chicken.

## Offensive weapon

The *striped skunk* is a night hunter that feeds on insects and small mammals. It spends most of the time by itself, and may share the burrow of a fox or raccoon. When threatened, the skunk turns its back on its enemy, raising its bushy tail, scratching with its front feet, and hissing loudly. If the enemy does not retreat, the skunk then sprays a stinking, stinging fluid from the anal gland in its bottom.

## Long-distance runner

Distinguished by its mournful howl, the *coyote* is a relative of the wolf. It lives alone and hunts at dusk, scavenging on carrion or eating jackrabbits, prairie dogs, and other rodents. It will sometimes hunt deer as a pack. Strong legs and a keen sense of smell help the pack follow prey for long distances and outrun it at speeds of 40 miles per hour (65 km/h). As the victim tires, the coyote moves in for the kill with its sharp-toothed jaws.

## Puffed up

The male *sage grouse* displays to rival males to win a territory and also a mate. He puffs out his breast, inflates air sacs in his neck, and makes popping calls. The winner attracts the female that is looking on. When they hatch, the young follow their mother, who teaches them to eat seeds and insects. It gets its name from the sagebrush plant on which it also feeds.

## Peep hole

The *burrowing owl* makes its home underground. It can dig with its feet and beak, but prefers to move into an abandoned prairie dog hole. It hunts mainly at night, swooping down on its prey from the air or from a perch. It eats rodents, insects, lizards, snakes, and birds. By day, it can be seen outside its burrow, but shelters inside if disturbed. It can turn its head through 180 degrees for all-round vision.

## Squirrel city

The *prairie dog* is in fact a burrowing squirrel. One male, a harem of females, and their young all live in a burrow as a family group, called a cotery. A network of tunnels connects the coteries into a huge underground city, home to thousands of animals. Their numbers are declining as their habitat is taken over for farms and other human uses.

## Suit of armor

The horny plates of the *common long-nosed armadillo* protect it from predators. If attacked, it lies flat with its legs tucked in, or rolls into a ball. A night-hunter, the armadillo trots around snuffling for roots or small animals, which it digs out with its long, curved claws. It also licks insects out of their nest holes with its sticky tongue.

## Saved from extinction

Great herds of *bison* once grazed their way across the prairies. But by 1880, nearly 60 million of these magnificent creatures had been shot by hunters and only 500 remained. Almost extinct, the bison were given protected grazing in national parklands, and today there are 25,000. Bison roam in herds of up to fifty animals and can live to be forty years old.

# WESTERN DESERTS

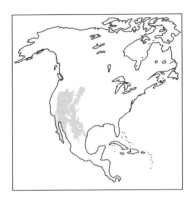

North America's desert regions extend from northern Mexico into the southwestern United States. The western deserts are parched, rocky, and barren. When it rains, the water rapidly evaporates or disappears into the ground. The deserts are also hot for much of the year. Death Valley, which is one of the hottest places on Earth, with temperatures of up to 129°F, is part of the western deserts. It links the Great Basin Desert to the more southerly Mojave Desert. South of the Mojave is the Sonoran Desert, famous for its giant saguaro cacti.

Most desert animals shelter during the day in burrows or under stones, cacti, or other plants, and come out at night to feed when it is cooler. Fruits, flowers, seeds—and the water-storing stems of cacti—provide both food and water for the insects and small mammals that can survive in the harsh desert environment. Plant-eating insects provide food for scorpions, spiders, and the trap-building antlion larva, as well as lizards and the elf owl. Small mammals that forage for seeds, such as rodents, are prey for the rattlesnake and a poisonous lizard called the gila monster. Larger plant eaters, such as jackrabbits and mule deer, are always alert to the approach of bobcats and other predators as they feed on tough grasses and cacti.

## Bony shell

The shell of the *desert tortoise* is made of bony plates fused together. The upper part is called the carapace, and the lower part is the plastron. The shell protects the animal from the desert sun. If threatened, the tortoise draws its head and legs back into its shell until the danger has passed. As it has no teeth, it tears at plants with the sharp edges of its jaws. It reproduces by laying eggs in the sand.

## Black-tailed jackrabbit

○ This is a hare that lives above ground, sheltering in a shallow scrape called a form.
○ Enormous ears give it acute hearing and act as a radiator to give off heat.
○ Males fight in spring for a mate.
○ To avoid predators, females hide young in different places.
○ Jackrabbits rarely drink water. They get moisture by nibbling succulent cacti.

## Antlion

○ So called because of its fierce larvae, which have huge mouthparts for grabbing prey.
○ Digs a pit in the sand and waits at the bottom for prey to tumble in.
○ Eats worms, caterpillars, ants, spiders, and centipedes.
○ Seizes prey with big, sawlike jaws, injects enzymes (proteins), and sucks out the juices.
○ Adult has long, delicate, lacy wings and feeds on insects.

## Gila monster

○ One of only two lizards with a poisonous bite.
○ Black and yellow coloring warns animals to stay away.
○ Produces poison in its lower jaw, which enters its victim as it bites and chews.
○ Eats other lizards, snakes, eggs, and small mammals and birds.
○ Heavy body and thick tail. Stores fat in its tail and lives off this when food is short.

## Roadrunner

○ Gets its name because it runs along roads and open ground in search of prey.
○ It can fly, but prefers to run. Reaching speeds of 19 miles per hour (30 km/h), it can run faster than most of its predators.
○ Tail is used as a brake and for steering.
○ When it catches a snake or lizard, it pecks it to death then swallows it headfirst.
○ Also eats insects and fruit.

## Hairy monster

Male *tarantulas* emerge from their shelter at dusk and wander the desert looking for food or a female. They mate in a burrow, where the female then lays her eggs. It can take ten years for a tarantula to grow into an adult. Like other spiders, it molts (sheds it skin) as it grows. It uses the poison in its bite to catch insects, then sucks the juices out from inside its prey. The hairs on the tarantula's body are irritating to predators and help deter them.

### Detective snake

The *western diamondback rattlesnake* finds its prey in different ways. Its eyes let in lots of light for good vision. It flicks out its forked tongue to taste the air for its prey. It has pit organs—heat-sensitive membranes between its eyes and nostrils. These detect slight changes in temperature that tell the snake the position of a warm-blooded animal.

# FLORIDA EVERGLADES

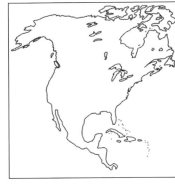

**The subtropical Everglades is the world's largest wetland. It is largely grass-covered marshland, dotted with ponds and islands of trees. The Everglades (mostly contained within a national park) covers about 2,300 square miles (6,000 km²) of the southern tip of the Florida peninsula. It provides a rich feeding and breeding area for many animals. The shallow fish-filled ponds, which are called 'gator holes because they are widened and deepened by American alligators, attract fish-eating water birds such as herons and spoonbills.**

The richness of animal life in the Everglades depends on the flooding that takes place after the dry winter months. In the north, heavy rains cause Lake Okeechobee to overflow, and this forms a river 6 inches (15 cm) deep and 50 miles (80 km) wide which covers the Everglades. As the runoff spreads, water levels rise and river animals move freely throughout the park. An explosion of wildlife, including insects and small fish, provides food for larger animals.

Among the many species living in the park are 150 species of fish, sixty species of amphibians and reptiles—including American alligators and crocodiles—and over 300 bird species, including the snail-eating Everglade kite and fish-eating osprey. The few mammal species include the endangered Florida panther and water-living manatee. As the marshes dry out in winter, the animals gather around the 'gator holes that are vital to the way the environment works. Unfortunately, the pressures caused by the expanding human population in southern Florida pose a serious threat to this wilderness.

## Glorious mud

The *American alligator* digs out the swamp to keep it flooded and well stocked with prey (freshwater turtles, fish, and snakes). Alligators mate in the water and the female lays her eggs in a mound of rotting vegetation. The eggs stay warm inside the mound and when the young hatch, the mother opens it up. The babies are independent from birth and are mature when they are 6½ feet (2 m) long, at about six years old.

## Sea cow

In the summer, *manatees* feed on the seagrass meadows of the Gulf of Mexico. In the fall, they migrate to the lagoons and estuaries of the Everglades and eat freshwater plants. Manatees are often called sea cows because of the way they graze underwater. They digest their food slowly and belch a lot. Manatees have poor eyesight, but they call to each other to keep in touch.

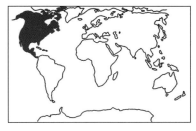

## Pink legs

Like flamingoes, the *roseate spoonbill* has pink legs and feathers because of its diet of shrimp and other shellfish. Flocks of spoonbills can be seen wading through the mangroves searching for food. They sweep their bills from side to side in the water, snapping up food by touch. They settle in colonies to breed, and build untidy nests in the treetops.

## Snail lover

The *Everglade kite* is also called the snail kite, because it feeds almost exclusively on just one type of water snail, the apple snail. It flies low over the water, watching out for snails clinging to the water plants, or spots its prey from a perch. Then it swoops and snatches the snail from the water with one of its feet. The Everglade kite holds the snail in its long, curling claws and uses its slender, hooked beak to scoop the creature from its shell. It nests in colonies and searches for food in groups.

## In the swim

The *anhinga* swims underwater with only its sharp bill and curved neck above water. It could be mistaken for a swimming snake, which is why it is also called the snakebird. The anhinga catches fish by spearing them on its bill, then brings them to the surface to swallow whole. After eating, it comes ashore to spread its wings and dry them in the sun.

## Under threat

For nine months of the year, floodwaters from Lake Okeechobee in the north fill the swamps and marshlands of the Everglades. But in the 1980s, a huge drainage program was begun, to take water from the lake for use in cities and to irrigate farmland. Now this unique environment and the many species that live there are under threat. Created a World Heritage Site in 1979, the Everglades is dependent on conservation efforts for its survival.

## Heat sensors

One of many water snakes that live in the Everglades, the *cottonmouth* is aggressive and dangerously poisonous. It belongs to the family of pit vipers. When hunting at night, it uses heat sensors situated in pits in its head to locate its prey. Also called the water moccasin, the cottonmouth eats fish, frogs, salamanders, other snakes, birds, and small mammals. It kills them with poisonous fangs.

# SOUTH AMERICA

South America is the world's fourth largest continent, with an area of about 6.9 million square miles (17.8m km²). Sitting between the Pacific and Atlantic Oceans, it extends over 4,300 miles (7,000 km), from tropical Panama —its link to North America—southward to the icy wastes of Cape Horn. Until two million years ago, South America was separate from North America and developed a unique set of animals, such as sloths, opossums, New World monkeys, and anteaters. South America also has the world's richest bird life. Around one-third of all bird species breed here and, including winter visitors, nearly half the world's bird species spend some time here. Over 700 species are unique to South America, including rheas, hoatzins, and antbirds.

The richest diversity of animals lives in the vast tract of tropical forest that covers the basin of the mighty Amazon River. These lush, dense forests in the north of the continent are home to millions of species, many of them insects and other invertebrates. Most of these have not yet been discovered or named. The Andes Mountains —the backbone of the continent—run down the west side, from Venezuela to Chile. Between the central section of the Andes and the Pacific is the hot Atacama Desert, one of the driest places on Earth—in some areas it has not rained for hundreds of years. Grasslands, including the pampas, fill much of the central and southern parts of South America.

## Andes

The *spectacled bear* is the only South American bear, and is named for the rings around its eyes. Each one has different "spectacles." Active at night, they live in the grasslands and humid forests on the lower slopes of the Andes. Excellent climbers, they use their large paws and strong claws to climb trees, tear off branches, climb back down, and eat the leaves and fruit. They sleep by day in a tree in a rough nest of sticks, or shelter in a den under a tangle of roots.

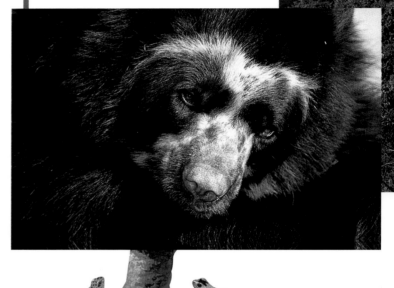

## Amazon

The brightly colored *poison dart frogs* are tropical forest-dwellers. Predators are warned off by their bold markings. Females lay eggs on wet leaves. When they hatch, the frogs carry the babies to pools inside cup-shaped bromeliads (which grow on trees), where they develop further. As the frogs grow, their colors develop and their skin starts to produce one of the deadliest known animal poisons. Amerindians can tip forty arrows with the poison from one frog, and this is how they get their name. Each arrow will paralyze an animal without making it dangerous to eat.

## Pampas

The *capybara* is the size of a pig and is related to the guinea pig. It has webbed feet and lives near water. In the heat of the day, it bathes in the shallows to cool off, emerging in late afternoon to graze. It also dashes into the water to escape from predators. Capybaras live in a family group with one male, who has a large black scent gland above his nose. He uses this to mark his territory during the breeding season, rubbing it against twigs and grass stems. Capybaras mate in the water, but are born on land. As the dry season approaches and pools shrink, they gather in herds of fifty to a hundred animals at permanent waterholes. Here, many young fall prey to hungry foxes and vultures.

Gulf of Venezuela

L. Maracaibo

GUYANA

VENEZUELA

SURINAM

FRENCH GUIANA

Cauca R.

Orinoco R.

Meta R.

Guyana Highlands

COLOMBIA

Malpelo

Branco R.

Marajo Island

Putumayo R.

ECUADOR

Negro R.

Amazon R.

ATLANTIC OCEAN

Gulf of Guayaquil

Amazon R.

Amazon Basin

Ucayali R.

Purus R.

Madeira R.

Tapajos R.

Xingu R.

Araguaia R.

Tocantins R.

Parnaiba R.

PERU

B R A Z I L

Brazilian Highlands

Andes

L. Titicaca

Sao Francisco R.

Plateau of Mato Grosso

BOLIVIA

Paraguay R.

Parana R.

PACIFIC OCEAN

Gran Chaco

PARAGUAY

Atacama Desert

Salado R.

Parana R.

Uruguay R.

Andes

ARGENTINA

URUGUAY

Pampas

River Plate

CHILE

Colorado R.

Negro R.

Valdes Peninsula

Gulf of San Jorge

Chico R.

Falkland Islands (UK)

Deseado R.

Tierra del Fuego

Cape Horn

| 0 | Miles | 1000 |
| 0 | Kilometers | 1600 |

# ANDES

The world's longest mountain chain, the Andes, runs for over 4,500 miles (7,250 km) down the western side of South America. The Andes have two parallel cordilleras (chains); the higher western peaks plunge steeply into the Pacific Ocean, while the eastern cordillera slopes more gently toward the Atlantic. The western slopes are dry, while the eastern have more rain, vegetation, and animals. Many peaks are snow-covered and always shrouded in mist; the highest—Aconcagua in Argentina—reaches 22,835 feet (6,960 m). Deforestation, cultivation, and overgrazing cause severe soil erosion, but national parks, such as the Manu in Peru, are going some way to reversing this.

The eastern slopes witness a dramatic change in climate, vegetation, and wildlife with increasing altitude. The lower slopes are covered in tropical forest, home to the spectacled bear, northern pudu, and the shy Andean tapir. Within several thousand feet, the hot, humid forest gives way to rocky slopes—home to the mountain viscacha—and then to snow-covered peaks. The two cordilleras are separated by a high plateau, or altiplano, covered by grassland or scrubland and dotted with lakes. The grasslands provide grazing for the vicuña, and for its domesticated relatives, the llama and alpaca. These and other high-altitude mammals are adapted for cold nights and for life in air that is low in oxygen. The lakes and wetlands of the altiplano are rich in fish and water birds.

## High flyer

Like all vultures, the *Andean condor* has a bald head and neck so it can feed deep in the carcasses of dead animals without getting its feathers bloody. The world's largest bird of prey, it has a wingspan of 10 1/2 feet (3.2 m). The condor soars on hot air currents high over the Andean foothills, looking for carrion. Its diet also includes fish. Because of poor food supply and poisoning by ranchers, the condor is getting scarce. The female lays only one egg at a time, and it takes two years to rear a chick.

## Andean flicker

○ A type of woodpecker that probes under bark for insects.
○ Catches ants on its long, sticky tongue.
○ Its feet are well adapted for climbing trees—two toes pointing forward and two backward to grip the bark.
○ Uses its beak to bore a nest hole in the puya plant. The puya has vicious spines, that provide dangerous but popular perches.

## Northern pudu

○ Smallest of the world's deer, only 15 inches (38 cm) high at its shoulder.
○ Lives in the lower Andean forests and in the swampy savanna that stretches across the mountain foothills.
○ Simple antlers, long coarse hair, and slender hooves.
○ Secretive animal that feeds on leaves, shoots, and fruit.
○ Females give birth to single calves or twins.

## Mountain viscacha

○ Looks like a long-tailed rabbit, and in some areas is called a "rock squirrel."
○ Found in dry, rocky terrain with sparse vegetation.
○ Families live in clefts and crevices in the rocks, forming colonies of up to seventy-five individuals.
○ Eats most plants including grasses, mosses, and lichens.
○ Very agile across the rocks, but stay close to home.

## Giant hummingbird

○ At 9 inches (23 cm) long, the largest of the world's hummingbirds.
○ Builds a tiny nest of mosses and lichens on top of a branch or on a cactus stem.
○ Hovering flight allows it to sip nectar from flowers while it is on the wing; also perches on branches to feed.
○ Can use its long beak to probe for insects in bark or among debris.

## Saved

The smallest member of the camel family, the *vicuña* grazes the high meadows of the Andes. Vicuñas were killed in large numbers for their valuable wool and hide, and, by 1965, only 6,000 remained in the wild. Recent conservation projects have saved the vicuña from extinction, and there are now about 85,000, mostly in national parks.

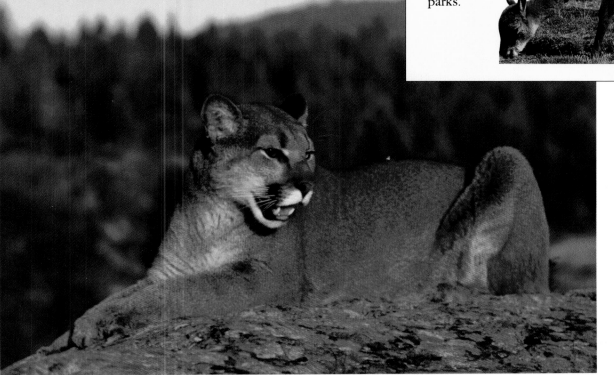

## Athlete

The *cougar* has many names, including puma, mountain lion, and panther. It lives all along the Andes and is also found in North America. It prowls alone through mountain forests and scrubland in search of prey such as brocket deer. A fearsome hunter, the cougar has remarkable jumping power—it can leap 20 feet (6 m) into a tree and cover more than 33 feet (10 m) in one bound on the ground.

# THE AMAZON RAIN FOREST

The Amazon rain forest of Brazil, Colombia, and northern Peru is the world's largest rain forest, covering nearly 2.3 million square miles (6m km²). It contains the greatest variety of animal life in the world, nearly half of all bird species—including 300 types of hummingbird—and an unknown number of insect species. The loud screeching of macaws fills the air, as do the booming calls of howler monkeys. Bright colors are everywhere, from the wings of butterflies to the warning patterns of poisonous frogs. The rain forest is hot, humid, and wet all year round, ideal for the many different species of trees, creepers, ferns, and epiphytes (plants that grow on trees), such as bromeliads.

The rich plantlife provides homes and food for the vast animal population. Each forest level has its own animal communities. Most live high in the canopy where the treetops are exposed to the sun. Here, flowers, fruit, leaves, and insects provide food for monkeys, fruit bats, hummingbirds, opossums, and toucans, all on the lookout for the fearsome harpy eagle. Lower down, snakes eat frogs and iguanas. Rainwater pools inside bromeliads provide drinking water and tadpole nurseries. On the forest floor, seed-eating rodents scuttle between the trees avoiding predators. The Amazon River and its tributaries are rich in life: Many fish eat fallen fruit, while piranhas eat fish and animals that come to the water to drink.

## Rare beauty

Ruthless hunting for their beautifully marked skin has wiped out *jaguars* in many areas. The jaguar hunts by stealth and ambush, mainly at night, feeding on anything from mice to tapirs. An excellent swimmer, it catches fish by flipping them out of the water with its paw. The jaguar lives alone, and males and females meet only to mate. Cubs stay near the den until they are about six months old, when they start to accompany their mother on hunting trips. After about three years, they can hunt for themselves and are independent. Jaguars, like all rain forest animals, are threatened by the loss of their habitat through fire, logging, and clearance for farming.

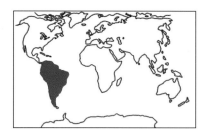

## Nutcracker

The largest of South American parrots, the *scarlet macaw* feeds on fruit and nuts, using its foot as a "hand" to hold its food. Its hooked beak is strong enough to crack the toughest nut of all, the Brazil —a food source unavailable to other birds. Macaws pair for life and bond by preening and "kissing."

## Stripper

*Piranhas* hunt by smell, and the scent of blood will drive them into a frenzy. They will attack a school of fish or any animal. Small fish are eaten whole. Piranhas use their needle-sharp teeth and strong jaws to tear chunks off larger prey—they can cut through bone in a single bite and strip all the flesh off an animal the size of a pig in a minute.

## Upside down

The *three-toed sloth* sleeps by day, eats leaves by night, mates, and gives birth, all hanging upside down in a tree by its long, hooked claws. It can turn its head through 270 degrees so that it can see all around without moving. The sloth is slow-moving and may live in the same tree for years, descending to the forest floor weekly to defecate. In the hot, humid forest, green algae grow on its fur, which helps to keep it camouflaged from predators.

## Blue jewel

The brilliant upper wings of the *blue morpho butterfly* flash as it takes off, startling any predators. Also, its patterned hind wings help to break up its

outline, so it is less of a target for hungry birds. The underside of its wings, displayed when it is at rest with its wings folded up, are dull brown. This camouflages the morpho, making it blend into the tree bark. The blue morpho is hunted by collectors for use in jewelry.

## Monkey-eater

The dominant bird of prey in the South American rain forest is the largest and most powerful eagle in the world, the *harpy eagle*. Up to 3 feet (1 m) from head to tail, the harpy eagle can reach speeds of up to 50 miles per hour (80 km/h) as it chases prey. It can carry off creatures as large as monkeys and sloths in its huge, powerful talons, and also feeds on opossums and snakes.

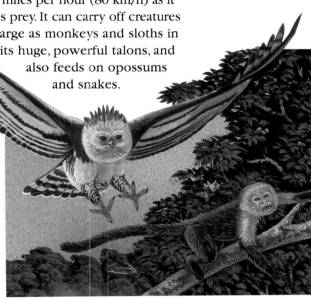

## Action needed

The destruction of the Amazon rain forest—for hardwood, mining, and farmland—could wipe out half the world's animal species, many native peoples, and a vast wealth of plants that may supply the cures for countless diseases. Burning the forest is also increasing levels of carbon dioxide gas in the atmosphere. At the current rate of destruction, no forest at all will be left by 2035.

# THE PAMPAS

East of the Andes, there are 500,000 square miles (1.3m km²) of temperate grassland, the best known area of which is the pampas of Argentina and Uruguay. The pampas once occupied over 166,000 square miles (430,000 km²). In the wetter eastern pampas, a lot of land has been taken over for grain farming. In the drier west, 300 years of cattle grazing has removed many of the native grasses, sedges, and shrubs. The pampas wildlife is not as rich as in the tropical forests, but it is home to many species that are found here and nowhere else. Many of these species are adapted to the open terrain. The few large plant grazers—apart from domesticated cattle—include the rare pampas deer.

Farther north, the water-loving capybara grazes on grasslands near water. Smaller grazers include the mara and viscacha, both related to the guinea pig. Like many smaller animals that have no trees or bushes to shelter in, they go underground. Other burrowers include insect-eating armadillos. Giant armadillos, which lash out with their sharp front claws if attacked, feed on termites. These insects live in massive colonies inside towering nests dotted around the pampas landscape. There are many ground-dwelling birds, like the rhea and the crested caracara. In addition to cougars, larger predators include the maned wolf, whose long legs enable it to see over tall grasses when hunting for prey.

## Blood feast

The fierce-looking *vampire bat* is not much bigger than a sparrow. It feeds mainly on the blood of cattle, pigs, and horses. Active by night, it bites its victim then laps blood from the wound. Its saliva stops the blood from clotting. The vampire bat is considered a pest by farmers since it can pass diseases like rabies to their livestock.

## Tight squeeze

The *boa constrictor* cannot catch fast-moving prey. It hunts by lying in wait or sliding silently up to its victim. It wraps its tail around the animal's body, constricting (squeezing) it, until it can no longer breathe. The boa's "elastic" jaws can open wide enough for it to eat a wild pig or a capybara whole. After a big meal, it will not need to eat for a week.

## Air-conditioned

*Termites* are soft-bodied insects that feed on plant material. They live in colonies in a termitarium (huge tower), which they build using a mixture of soil and saliva that sets like cement. At the heart of the colony lives a bloated, egg-laying queen. Workers build food stores, air shafts, fungus gardens, and passages to the outside world. These are guarded by sentries, which let workers in and out.

## Ruffled feathers

The tousled plumage of the *rhea* is one sign that this bird cannot fly —only flying birds need a streamlined shape.

Another clue is the long, muscular legs, well-adapted to racing across grasslands to outpace predators. The male mates with several females, then builds a nest in which they lay their eggs. He incubates the eggs and rears the young, caring for them for up to five months. Rheas eat seeds, insects, and small animals.

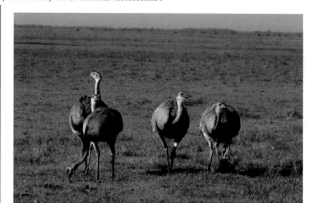

## Sprinter

The *mara* is also called the Patagonian hare, but it is in fact a rodent. It can leap 6 feet (about 2 m) and runs at 28 miles per hour (45 km/h) to escape its predators. It feeds by day on grass, shoots, leaves, and fruit. The mara digs its own burrow or takes one over from another animal, like the viscacha. Mara numbers are declining, particularly where a competitor, such as the introduced European hare, is found.

## Home-wrecker

The *giant anteater* feeds on ants and termites. Its tongue, which is covered in spines and saliva to trap insects, extends about 2 feet (60 cm)—over half its body length. A giant anteater needs to eat 30,000 insects a day and may visit forty nests. It tears open a termite mound with its huge claws but does not destroy it, so it can return to feed again. The anteater protects its claws by walking on its knuckles.

## Competition

The animals of the pampas now compete with grazing herds of livestock, particularly beef cattle, for their food. Intensive farming with too many cattle in small areas of pasture has led to overgrazing and damage to the pampas ecology. Farmers protecting their herds and pastures with guns are an added threat. As ranching has increased, many native animal species have disappeared, including the jaguar. Other species, including the giant anteater, are frequently shot on sight even though they are not pests or of any commercial value.

# AUSTRALASIA

**Australasia includes Australia, New Zealand, and the surrounding islands, as well as Papua New Guinea (the eastern half of the island of New Guinea). Lying between the Indian and Pacific Oceans, Australia is the world's smallest continent, with an area of under 3 million**

## Tropical North

The *spotted cuscus* is a tree-living marsupial from the rain forests of New Guinea and the Australian north. It feeds at night on leaves, flowers, and fruit, and also eats small reptiles and birds. An excellent climber, the cuscus clings to the branches with its feet and its prehensile (gripping) tail. During the day, it rests high up in the trees, hiding from predators.

**square miles (7.7m km². Australia has been isolated for some 30 million years and has many unique animals, including the world's greatest variety of marsupial, or pouched, mammals such as kangaroos and koalas. Marsupials, found also in New Guinea and the Americas, give birth to tiny, underdeveloped young that must complete their development in their mother's pouch. Australia also has as a wide range of birds, reptiles, insects, and spiders.**

Australia is mostly hot, dry desert, grassland, and scrub, known collectively as the outback. Marsupial mice, emus, and wallabies are adapted to these hot, dry conditions. To the east of the Great Dividing Range, the climate is milder, with hot summers and cooler winters. New Guinea and northeastern Australia have tropical forests. A rich variety of animals live here, like the cuscus and tree kangaroo. New Zealand has a warm, wet climate with few native mammals. Introduced species like rabbits, cats, and foxes have affected and wiped out some of Australasia's native wildlife.

## Outback

The *brown falcon* hunts by watching motionless from a high perch, then swooping down on its prey. With its long legs and broad wings, it is one of the biggest falcons, but it tackles small prey. It feeds on small mammals, reptiles, insects, and young or injured birds, gripping them with its powerful talons and ripping their flesh with its beak. It has a harsh, cackling call, and the females are larger than the males.

## Great Barrier Reef

The *wobbegong*, or carpet shark, lurks on the seabed, waiting to feed. It is camouflaged by its mottled brown, gray, and yellow coloring and by the protrusions (growths) around its mouth. When a small fish swims nearby, the wobbegong makes a sudden lunge forward and sucks its prey into its mouth. It has two to five rows of small, razor-sharp teeth. These do not pierce the prey deeply, but clamp down hard on it so that it cannot escape.

INDIAN
OCEAN

*Timor
Sea*

*Arafura Sea*

Torres Strait

PAPUA
NEW GUINEA

*Central Range*

*Bismarck Sea*

New Ireland

Bougainville

SOLOMON
ISLANDS

New
Britain

Choiseul

New
Georgia

Cape
York

*Gulf of
Carpentaria*

*Coral
Sea*

Arnhem
Land

Kimberley
Plateau

*Fitzroy R.*

Great Sandy Desert

N o r t h e r n
T e r r i t o r y

*Great Barrier Reef*

*Great Dividing Range*

A U S T R A L I A

Q u e e n s l a n d

Gibson Desert

Macdonnell
Ranges

Simpson
Desert

*Fraser
Island*

*Western
Australia*

Great Victoria
Desert

*L. Eyre*

S o u t h
A u s t r a l i a

*Darling R.*

N e w
S o u t h
W a l e s

*Australian Alps*

*Great Australian
Bight*

*Kangaroo
Island*

*Murray R.*

V i c t o r i a

*Bass Strait*

*Tasman
Sea*

T a s m a n i a

| 0 | Miles | 1000 |
|---|-------|------|
| 0 | Kilometers | 1600 |

# New Zealand

The bold, inquisitive *kea* is the only meat-eating parrot. It is named after its call, "kee-ah." It is heavily built and can be seen near houses and farms, where it feeds on small mammals and dead animals, using its long, hooked beak to rip the flesh. It is a powerful flier, but spends a lot of time on the ground, scratching for grubs and insects. It also eats seeds, leaves, nectar, and fruit. It makes its nest in a rocky crevice and lines it with grass, twigs, and chewed wood. The young form flocks, but adult males live in a territory with up to four females.

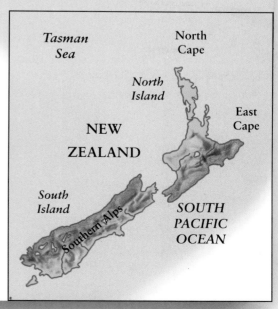

*Tasman
Sea*

North
Cape

*North
Island*

East
Cape

NEW
ZEALAND

*South
Island*

*Southern Alps*

SOUTH
PACIFIC
OCEAN

67

# THE TROPICAL NORTH

## AUSTRALASIA

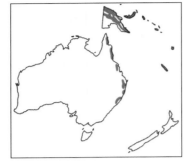

The northeastern part of Australia and mountainous New Guinea—the island some 1,370 miles (2,200 km) long that lies off its coast—share the same hot and wet climate and the same rain forest vegetation. The many species of ferns and trees found in the forest provide homes and food for a huge array of unusual animals. Australia's rain forests cover only 0.1 percent of the continent, yet contain 30 percent of its frogs, two of the three species of monotreme (egg-laying mammal), 30 percent of its marsupials, 62 percent of its butterflies, and a large proportion of its bats, birds, and reptiles, including the deadly poisonous taipan snake.

Much of the forest is now protected as a World Heritage Site, which is intended to prevent wholesale destruction in the future. However, the introduction of alien species, such as the cane toad, has affected native animals, such as the carnivorous quoll, which is poisoned by the toad's skin secretions.

The rain forests of New Guinea and Australia have a rich variety of canopy-living animals, including brightly colored lorikeets and cuscuses, which feed on fruit, flowers, and leaves, as well as sugar gliders—marsupials that glide from tree to tree.

## Bright camouflage

The bright green male *eclectus parrot* and the red and blue female were once thought to be different species. Their brilliant plumage provides excellent camouflage in the colorful canopy of New Guinea's rain forest. The male is difficult to spot in the treetops, searching for nuts, fruits, and seeds. The female disappears into the shadows as she incubates her eggs in a nest hole in a tree.

## Hard hat

A flightless *cassowary* uses its small wings to help it balance while running and for breeding time displays. Instead of feathers, the wings are covered in bare quills. It has a bony crest, called a casque; this protects its head when it runs through the undergrowth to escape predators. The female may pair with more than one male, laying a clutch of eggs for each. The boldly striped chicks are cared for by their father for nine months.

## Climbing marsupial

The *tree kangaroo* is well adapted to life in rain forest trees. It has shorter hind legs and longer forelegs than its ground-dwelling relative. Its sharp, curved claws and the rough pads under its feet are used for gripping tree bark. Its long tail helps it to balance and steer as it scrambles and leaps through the trees in search of juicy leaves and fruit. It is active at night; by day, it curls up to sleep on a branch.

## Flower power

*Southern blossom bats* use their tongue to feed on flower nectar and pollen, which showers down on them and sticks to their fur. Visiting another flower of the same species, they rub against it and pollination occurs. Unlike insect-eating bats that rely on echolocation to find prey, blossom bats and other fruit bats use their nose and eyes to lead them to food.

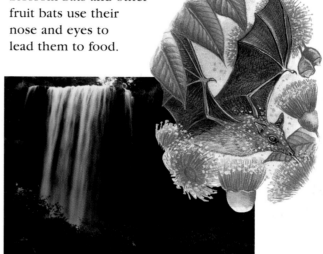

## Deadly venom

One of the world's most poisonous snakes, the *taipan* injects deadly venom deep into its prey with its ½ inch (1 cm) fangs. Taipans are shy and solitary and rarely seen. In winter, they lie coiled up in sheltered dens. The female taipan lays her eggs in a hollow in soft soil and leaves them to hatch. Within days of hatching, the young snake kills its first prey.

## Jewel of the forest

The *Raggiana* is the most spectacular of New Guinea's forty birds of paradise. The males compete high in a rain forest tree. They flap their wings frantically, toss their spectacular display feathers, and hang upside down in a shimmering frenzy. The female chooses the showiest bird to be her mate. Normally, just one or two dominant males do all the matings; the other males in the lek (display area) display in vain.

## Bad mistake

The *cane toad* was introduced into Australia from South America in 1935 to eat cane beetles destroying the sugarcane plantations, but the experiment backfired. The toads failed to wipe out the beetles and became pests themselves, by eating native species including snakes, frogs, small mammals, and birds. Cane toad numbers have increased rapidly because they have no natural enemies. Also, any animal that touches or attempts to eat the toad is poisoned by the toxic secretions released from glands behind its head.

# THE OUTBACK

**Most of Australia's people live on the coast, especially in the east and southeast. Of the rest of the country, nearly half is hot desert, and over a third is scrub or dry grassland—hot in summer and cool in winter—which surrounds the central desert. Together, these vast areas form the outback, a dry plateau that stretches from the west coast to the eastern mountains. In the outback, water is in short supply. Despite the harsh conditions, a wide range of animals thrives here, although only a fraction of the number found in Australia's eastern forests. Many survive on little or no water, and seek shelter during the day from the sun.**

In the outback, drought-resistant plants like porcupine grass and acacia trees provide shelter and food for animals. There are many reptiles, such as goannas, skinks, frilled lizards, and the bizarre-looking thorny devil, whose spiny skin gathers water droplets from the morning dew. Birds such as cockatoos and parakeets fly in flocks between scattered trees. The mammals range from meat-eating marsupial "mice," such as dunnarts and mulgaras, to kangaroos and wallabies. Where grasslands are used for grazing by farmers, the vast herds of cattle and sheep compete for food with the native grazers. Introduced species, such as foxes and feral cats, have caused the extinction of some native marsupial species.

## Gone wild

A member of the dog family and once a pet of the Aborigines, the *dingo* has been wild for many years. It is now regarded as a pest, as it sometimes preys on livestock. Family groups have a core territory, but may hunt over a wide area in a pack. After the dingoes have eaten their fill, they bury the leftover carcass for later.

## Marsupial mouse

Dunnarts are sometimes called marsupial mice because of their size and pointed face. But, unlike mice, the *fat-tailed dunnart* eats insects and spiders caught during nighttime hunts. In the wet season, it builds up food reserves in its tail. In the dry season, when food is scarce, the tail shrinks as the dunnart uses up its reserves. In a long drought, it rests under logs or rocks to make its food stores last longer.

## Bouncy

*Red kangaroos* travel in mobs (groups) of up to 100, move at up to 35 miles per hour (56 km/h), and can hop nearly 40 feet (12 m) in a single bound. They graze, mainly on grass, resting on their shorter front feet. They usually feed and travel at night, with mothers carrying their young, called joeys, in their pouch. By day, they rest sheltering from the sun.

70

## Spiny egg-layer

The short-beaked *echidna* has no teeth or jaw muscles. It feeds by licking up ants and other insects with its sticky tongue. The echidnas and the duck-billed platypus are the only mammals that lay eggs. The female lays a single egg in a pouch on her abdomen. The baby hatches out of the leathery shell and feeds on her milk for about two months.

## Big ruff

The *frilled lizard* uses surprise tactics to scare away enemies. It opens a colored parasol of skin around its neck. This makes it look much bigger than it is. At the same time, it bobs its head with its mouth open to show the bright color inside, hisses, and lashes about with its tail. This can scare away predators such as the gray goshawk.

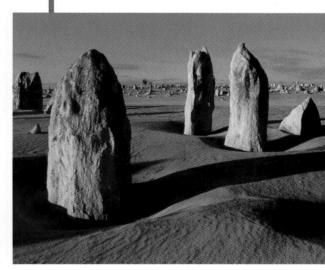

## Blue neck

The flightless *emu* is Australia's biggest bird and can be 5 ½ feet (1.7 m) tall. Its tiny wings are hidden under its long feathers and it strides around on long, muscular legs. The male has a low, booming mating call. The female lays her eggs in a hollow in the ground, and the male cares for the chicks. In some areas, the emu has become a pest. It eats almost anything and can trample sheep fences.

## Protected

The *koala* was once hunted for its fur and faced extinction. Now it is protected and lives in the forests of eastern Australia. Koalas eat only eucalyptus leaves. There are more than 100 species of eucalyptus in Australia, but koalas will feed on only twelve of them.
A koala eats about 2 pounds (1 kg) of not-very-nutritious leaves a night; during the day it rests for eighteen hours to save energy. The koala's worst enemy is forest fire.

# THE GREAT BARRIER REEF

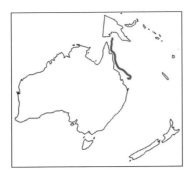

The Great Barrier Reef is the largest coral reef in the world and can be seen from space. It extends for 1,250 miles (2,000 km), from Papua New Guinea to the Tropic of Capricorn, off Australia's northeastern coast. Reefs grow in shallow tropical seas. A reef consists of the protective, chalky skeletons of tiny coral organisms related to sea anemones, called polyps. It takes hundreds of years for a reef to form. Polyps have two sources of food: They use their stinging tentacles to catch prey that floats past in the reef's currents, and they contain tiny plantlike algae, which make food from sunlight. Coral reefs are rich in animal life because they provide plentiful food, shelter, and a place to breed.

The Great Barrier Reef contains over 400 species of coral, including brain corals, stag corals, and delicate fan corals. Around 1,500 species of fish live here. The moray eel lies in wait for prey in coral crevices—other fish swim in large schools, feeding on plankton and algae. Sharks patrol the reef, waiting for a fish to move away from its shelter. The reef also has over 4,000 species of mollusk, including sea slugs and octopuses that lurk in crevices before grabbing prey with their tentacles. Sea urchins, turtles, and sea cucumbers are also common. The reef's status as a World Heritage Site should protect it from the damage done by tourists and divers who threaten reefs around the world.

## Supershell

One of the world's largest invertebrates, at 880 pounds (400 kg) and over 3 feet (1 m) long, is the *giant clam*. It lives in the shallows of the tropical Pacific Ocean. Its shell opens to feed, and shuts quickly when danger approaches. The opened shell is fringed by brightly colored soft tissue. Its vivid greens and blues are produced by algae that form a relationship with the clam. The clam "farms" the algae and gets nutrients from them, as well as filtering food particles from the water. The algae have a home in which to grow, reproduce, and photosynthesize using the sun's rays.

## Long meal

The flattened tail of the *olive sea snake* acts like a powerful paddle to thrust it through the water after its prey. The female is larger than the male and feeds mainly on the bigger eels that live in deep water off the reef. The smaller males hunt for moray eels in the reef face. Their venom stuns their prey, which they then eat whole.

## Clownfish

○ Has a special relationship with sea anemones and is immune to the sting in the anemone's tentacles.

○ When pursued by an enemy, it hides among the anemone's tentacles, which sting and devour its predator. Clownfish eats the leftovers.

○ Chases away butterfly fish, which prey on the anemone, by biting off the ends of its tentacles.

○ Cleans debris off the anemone and eats dead tentacles.

## Brain coral

○ So called because it looks like a human brain—one of many types that make up the Great Barrier Reef.

○ Corals are the hollow skeletons of thousands of tiny animals, called polyps, which live together in colonies. These skeletons build up to form a reef.

○ A polyp looks like a sea anemone, with a ring of stinging tentacles that wave in the water to catch food.

## Blue-streaked cleaner wrasse

○ So called because it removes parasites from other fish.

○ Bright coloring and swimming pattern attract the larger fish that it cleans.

○ Fish wait in line for the cleaner's services.

○ Large predators like the moray eel allow the cleaner wrasse to remove debris from between their teeth without harming it.

○ Also rids larger fish of dead or diseased tissue.

## Tiger shark

○ Cruises off the reef, feeding on any marine prey. Sometimes presents a threat to divers exploring the reef.

○ Also feeds on sea snakes.

○ Jaws are loosely attached to its skull, so it can open them wide to take huge bites out of its prey with its razor-sharp teeth.

○ Worn-out teeth are continuously replaced by rows of newer ones.

○ May use as many as 30,000 teeth in a lifetime.

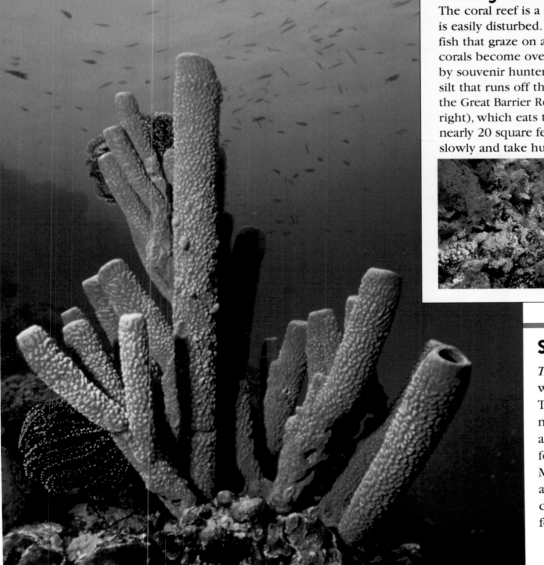

## Endangered

The coral reef is a fragile habitat and its complex food web is easily disturbed. Reefs are threatened by overfishing. If the fish that graze on algae growing on the reef are removed, the corals become overgrown. Reefs worldwide are also damaged by souvenir hunters, boats, and pollution, and smothered by silt that runs off the land. Much damage has been caused to the Great Barrier Reef by the *crown of thorns starfish* (below right), which eats the coral polyps. One starfish can destroy nearly 20 square feet (1.8 m²) of coral in a day. Coral reefs grow slowly and take hundreds of years to recover from damage.

## Softie

*Tubular sponges* live on parts of the reef where there is plenty of food for them. They draw in water and filter out the nutrients. Branching varieties of sponge are found in still waters; more rounded forms grow where tides are stronger. Many small creatures thrive in and around sponges, such as tiny brittle stars, crustaceans, and worms, which feed on the food particles the sponge draws into itself.

# NEW ZEALAND & TASMANIA

Mixed forest
Mountain
Rainforest
Scrubland

New Zealand is 1,000 miles (1,600 km) east of Australia, halfway between the South Pole and the equator. There are two main islands—North and South—with smaller islands around them. The overall climate is mild, but part of North Island is subtropical, while parts of South Island have heavy snow in winter, and glaciers and fjords mark the landscape. Rich farmland is found on both islands. New Zealand became isolated about 80 million years ago, well before Australia, and before mammals became widely distributed. Therefore it has only two native species of mammals—both are bats. Without predators, many birds such as kiwis, takahes, keas, and kakapos became flightless. Unfortunately, European settlers brought predators with them in the shape of rats, cats, and dogs, and many native ground-dwelling birds are now found only in isolated areas or on small islands.

## NEW ZEALAND

### Big egg

The flightless *kiwi* forages at night in dense undergrowth. Unusually for a bird, it uses smell to find food, sniffing out grubs, insects, and spiders with the nostrils at the end of its beak. It lays the biggest egg relative to its size of any bird. The male sits on the egg in his burrow for up to twelve weeks. After the incubation, the baby kiwi hatches and is ready to forage for food with its parents within a week.

Tasmania, the wettest and most mountainous part of Australia, lies 150 miles (240 km) off its southeastern coast. Like New Zealand and Australia, its native animals have suffered from the arrival of settlers and their animals. But it still has a wide range of marsupials, such as quolls and wombats, as well as the egg-laying platypus. The Tasmanian devil is also found here. Mystery surrounds the existence of the thylacine, the largest meat-eating marsupial. Once hunted near to extinction, it may have been wiped out by disease earlier last century, or—perhaps—a few may survive in isolated areas. The search goes on.

### Living fossil

The *tuatara* is the sole survivor of a reptile group that lived alongside the dinosaurs. Today, it is found on only a few small islands. The female lays five to fifteen eggs that hatch in fifteen months. The young grow slowly and can live for 120 years. Tuatara means "peaks on the back"—males raise these spines when alarmed. They shelter in burrows by day and hunt at night for worms, insects, and spiders.

### Surfers

At dusk in the breeding season, *fairy penguins* ride ashore on the surf, then waddle up the beach to join their chicks and mates in their burrows. The adults take turns to stay in the nest and go to sea to feed on fish and squid. They breed on the shores of New Zealand, Australia, and Tasmania. They are fast and agile underwater, sometimes working together to round up schools of small fish.

# TASMANIA

## Egg-laying mammal

Living beside quiet waterways in Tasmania and Australia, the *duck-billed platypus* is an excellent swimmer that forages underwater for crayfish, freshwater shrimps, and insect larvae. It probes for prey in the stream bed using its sensitive bill. The female platypus makes a nest in the riverbank at the end of a long burrow and lines it with grasses. She lays two eggs. The young are 1 inch (2.5 cm) long when they hatch. They suckle milk from their mother, and stay in the burrow until they are ready to fend for themselves.

## Little demon

The size of a small dog, the *Tasmanian devil* is named because of its black coat and eerie wail and because it makes its prey disappear by eating every scrap. It has short, strong legs for foraging for reptiles and small mammals, and its powerful jaws and sharp teeth can crush bones. It also eats dead sheep and wallabies.

## Hunting party

Now very rare, the *eastern quoll* is found in the dry forests of Tasmania. Emerging at night from a daytime home in a rock pile or hollow log, it hunts for small insects, birds, reptiles, and rodents. The female quoll gives birth to up to twenty-four tiny young, but only the strongest survive. When they are older, they cling to her body and ride with her when she goes hunting.

## Teeth that grow

Wombats live in burrows up to 65 feet (20 m) long and are active at night. The female carries her baby in a pouch that faces backward. At six months, the wombat climbs out of its mother's pouch and forages with her for roots, grasses, and fungi. Wombats have long, sharp teeth that grow continually as they get worn down by cropping the vegetation.

# ANTARCTICA

The size of Europe and the United States combined, Antarctica is the windiest, coldest, driest, and most isolated continent on Earth. During the long, dark winter, temperatures can drop to -128°F, and the wind can gust at 125 miles per hour (200 km/h). Antarctica is surrounded by seas and buried under a permanent ice cap 3 miles (4.8 km) thick in places, which contains 90 percent of the world's ice (70 percent of its fresh water). The icecap extends over the ocean as sheets that retreat in summer and expand in winter. Only 2 percent of Antarctica is ice-free and it is here that its only permanent residents— a few insects and mites—live.

However, the ocean around Antarctica teems with life, especially during the short summer. An upwelling of nutrients around the coast encourages the growth of phytoplankton (tiny plant plankton) that float near the surface. These provide food for zooplankton— especially shrimplike krill—which feed crab, fish, and squid. These are eaten by seals and penguins and they, in turn, are eaten by killer whales and leopard seals. Krill is also an important food for baleen whales like the blue whale. Many seals and seabirds take up temporary residence on land in summer to molt and breed. Current agreements protect Earth's last unspoiled wilderness by forbidding mining or oil exploration. But commercial fishing for krill—a major food source —could easily upset the fragile ocean ecosystem.

## Giant bird

With a 10-foot (3-m) wingspan, the *wandering albatross* is a powerful flier. It masters southern ocean storms, soaring hundreds of miles in search of squid. It stores food as an oily liquid in its stomach to be digested later or regurgitated for its chick. It nests in small colonies on Antarctic islands and pairs for life, normally rearing one chick every two years. It matures after ten years and can live for thirty years.

## Footsie

*Emperor penguins* breed on the winter ice surrounding Antarctica. The female lays a single egg, which the male incubates balanced on his feet for about sixty days. His mate goes to sea to feed. The males huddle together to withstand the cold. The female returns and feeds the chick with regurgitated fish. The male can then feed. At about three months, the chicks gather next to the water while both adults fetch food.

## Fast mover

*Adélie penguins* eat krill and fish. To leave the water, they swim to shore and leap up to 10 feet (3 m) to land on the ice on their feet or stomach. Using their feet and flippers, they toboggan over the ice. Adélie penguins nest onshore in summer, in crowded colonies, each bird returning to the same mate and nest every year and rearing two young.

## Dainty eater

The largest creature ever to have lived on the planet, the *blue whale* feeds in the summer months on krill. Instead of teeth, its mouth has rows of baleen plates fringed with bristles. The whale gulps in water, then forces it back out so that the baleen bristles strain out the tiny prey, which it then swallows. In the fall, the whales move to warmer waters and do not eat for up to eight months.

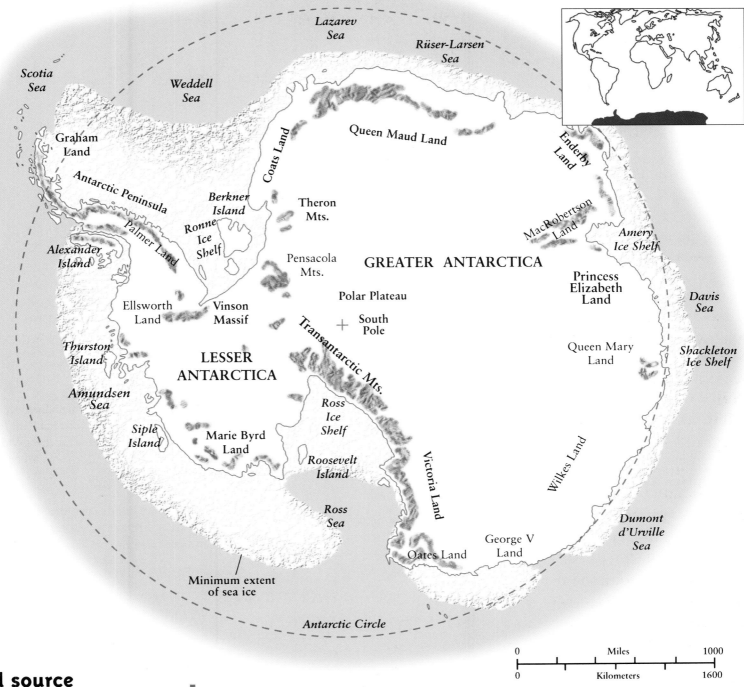

Lazarev
Sea

Rüser-Larsen
Sea

Scotia
Sea

Weddell
Sea

Graham
Land

Antarctic Peninsula

Coats Land

Queen Maud Land

Enderby
Land

Berkner
Island

Theron
Mts.

Ronne
Ice
Shelf

Palmer Land

MacRobertson
Land

Amery
Ice Shelf

Alexander
Island

Pensacola
Mts.

GREATER ANTARCTICA

Princess
Elizabeth
Land

Davis
Sea

Ellsworth
Land

Vinson
Massif

Polar Plateau

+ South
Pole

Queen Mary
Land

Shackleton
Ice Shelf

Thurston
Island

LESSER
ANTARCTICA

Transantarctic Mts.

Amundsen
Sea

Ross
Ice
Shelf

Siple
Island

Marie Byrd
Land

Roosevelt
Island

Victoria Land

Wilkes Land

Ross
Sea

Dumont
d'Urville
Sea

Minimum extent
of sea ice

Oates Land

George V
Land

Antarctic Circle

| 0 | | Miles | | 1000 |
| 0 | | Kilometers | | 1600 |

# Food source

*Krill* are finger-length, shrimplike creatures. In summer, they are found close to the ocean's surface in swarms of many millions. Krill feed on plankton, filtering them out of the water with their feathery front legs. In turn, they provide food for many other creatures, such as the blue whale, which eats up to 8,800 pounds (4,000 kg) of krill a day. Krill breed quickly in these nutrient-rich waters. One female can lay 3,000 eggs a year.

# Foghorn

The largest seal in the world, a male *southern elephant seal* can weigh up to 8,800 pounds (4,000 kg). Elephant seals feed on fish and squid and can dive as deep as 5,000 feet (1,500 m). In the breeding season, each high-ranking male guards a harem of up to 100 females. The male roars at rival males to stay away, amplifying the sound through the inflatable skin bag on his nose. If threats fail, the male will fight his rival.

# Spotted hunter

The *leopard seal* patrols the edge of the pack ice. A ferocious hunter and a fast swimmer, it eats penguins, fish, krill, seals, and their pups. Leopard seals spend most of their time in the freezing waters and have a thick layer of blubber that keeps them warm. They come to the surface to breathe and keep their nostrils open by scraping the ice off with their teeth.

# GLOSSARY

**Algae** Simple plantlike living things, most of which live in water.

**Amphibian** Vertebrate that lives both on land and in water.

**Arachnid** Arthropod with four pairs of legs, such as a spider or scorpion.

**Arthropod** Invertebrate with jointed hard outer skeleton and limbs.

**Backbone** Flexible chain of bones that runs from head to tail in a vertebrate.

**Baleen** Fringed plates that hang from the roof of the mouth of the largest whales and filter their food.

**Biodiversity** Variety of living things in one area.

**Biome** Area such as savanna or tropical forest defined by its climate, plant life, and associated animals.

**Biosphere** All regions on Earth—land, air, and sea—inhabited by living things.

**Camouflage** Colors, patterns, and shapes that make an animal hard to see against its background.

**Canopy** Top layer of branches and leaves that form the "roof" of a forest.

**Carnivore** Meat eater.

**Carrion** Dead animal eaten by scavengers.

**Classification** Method of identifying and grouping animals.

**Climate** Average weather conditions found in a particular region.

**Colony** Members of the same species that live together and interact.

**Conifer** Tree such as pine that reproduces by making seeds in cones.

**Coral** Tiny marine colonial polyps that produce a protective outer casing; over centuries these produce a coral reef.

**Crustacean** Arthropod such as lobster or crab with jointed legs and two pairs of antennae (feelers).

**Deciduous** Describes a tree that sheds its leaves in the fall.

**Desert** An area where very little rain falls, so few plants can grow.

**Drought** A long period without rain.

**Echolocation** System used by bats to determine the position of an object using timing and direction of echoes.

**Ecology** Study of relationship between living things and their environment.

**Ecosystem** The community of different animal and plant species found in a particular habitat.

**Endothermic** Describes animals— birds and mammals—whose bodies are kept at a constant warm temperature.

**Food chain** Food pathway linking different species in an ecosystem; energy flows along a food chain from plants to plant eaters to meat eaters.

**Food web** Food chains linked together within an ecosystem.

**Genus** Group of one or more closely related species.

**Gland** An organ in an animal that produces chemicals. Some mammals have scent glands that give off a strong smell, used for marking territory.

**Habitat** Place where a species lives.

**Herbivore** Plant eater.

**Hibernation** Sleeplike state used by some mammals to survive the cold winter months.

**Incubate** To sit on eggs and keep them warm until they hatch.

**Invertebrate** Animal without a backbone.

**Larva** The young of certain animals. Caterpillars are the larvae (plural) of butterflies.

**Mammal** Endothermic animal that has a covering of fur and feeds its young on milk. Most mammals give birth to well-developed young.

**Marsupial** Mammals that give birth to tiny, undeveloped young that grow inside a pouch.

**Mating** The coming together of a male and a female animal for reproduction.

**Metamorphosis** Change from one state into another as an animal develops into an adult, e.g. from a tadpole into a frog.

**Migrate** To travel from one area to another to find more favorable conditions, e.g. food.

**Mollusk** Soft-bodied invertebrate like a snail, often with a hard protective shell.

**Monotreme** Egg-laying mammal.

**Pampas** Grasslands of South America.

**Photosynthesis** The process by which plants make food using sunlight.

**Placental** Describes mammals that give birth to well-developed young.

**Pollination** Transfer of pollen from the male part of a flower to the female part; necessary for sexual reproduction and seed production.

**Polyp** Small tube-shaped animal with tentacles around its mouth; single polyps include sea anemones, colonial forms include the Portuguese man-of-war.

**Prairie** North American grasslands.

**Predator** Animal that hunts other animals for food.

**Reproduction** The production of offspring (young).

**Reptile** Vertebrate with waterproof scaly skin, such as a lizard, that typically lays eggs and lives on land.

**Rodent** A mammal with sharp incisors (front teeth) for gnawing, such as a mouse or squirrel.

**Savanna** Hot grasslands in Africa.

**Scavenger** Animal that feeds on the carcasses of other animals.

**Species** Group of similar living things that breed together in the wild.

**Steppe** Grasslands of Central Europe and Asia.

**Taiga** Northern coniferous forest of Europe and Asia.

**Temperate** A climate that does not have extremely hot summers or extremely cold winters.

**Tentacle** The "arm" of an animal, such as an octopus, used for grasping.

**Territory** Area defended by an animal where it feeds and breeds.

**Tropics** The region of Earth around the equator, which has a warm, wet climate all year round.

**Tundra** Land around the North Pole where the ground is frozen all year.

**Tusk** Tooth that sticks out of the jaw.

**Venom** Poison injected by one animal into another through fangs or a sting.

**Vertebrate** Animal with a backbone.

# INDEX

Abbreviations: t-top, m-middle, b-bottom, r-right, l-left, c-center

**Artwork credits:** Map artwork—Stephen Sweet. 4b, 5bl, 7mr, 7br, 7br, 8mt, 10bm, 19mt, 22ml, 23tl, 23mr, 23br, 24bl, 25tl, 25t, 25tm, 25tr, 25bm, 29br, 29tm, 33ml, 40m, 41br, 46bl, 47bl, 54mt, 61tr, 68m, 69tr, 69tl, 69br, 72b, 73tr, 73ml, 75br, 75bm, 76br, 77br - Terry Riley. 7ml, 7m, 29tr, 49m, 49mr, 49ml, 49br, 64bl, 65bl, 65mr, 65br, 76bl—Andrew Tewson. 7m, 7mr, 26br, 27br, 32bm, 32bl, 35ml, 40bl, 43ml, 61tm, 61tl, 70br - Dave Burroughs. 7ml, 7mr, 7mr, 8m, 8ml, 9bl, 9bm, 14br, 14bl, 18m, 18bl, 20m, 44bl, 44br, 45ml, 45bl, 45br, 66tm, 66mr, 67bm - Stan Peach. 16tm, 16bm, 19m, 19bl, 57m, 57mr - Rob Shone. 7ml, 30br, 31ml, 31bl, 31mr, 36mr, 51mr, 51br, 53ml, 53bl, 53mr—Stephen Angel. 7tr - Dan Woods. Additional artwork by: Peter Barrett, James Field, Karen Johnson, Ian Moores, Jonathon Pointer, John Rignall, Chris Shields, Michael Taylor, Myke Taylor, George Thompson.

**Photograph credits:** 1, 7tl, 7tm, 7mlr, 11bl, 16t, 17bl, 25mr, 33t, 33mt, 62, 63mt—John Foxx Images. 2, 7rb, 8br, 36t, 38l, 38r, 39tl, 44 both, 45tr, 55l, 66c, 66bl, 67, 68mr, 68br, 69ml, 70l, 70bl, 71tl, 71mr—Corbis. 7cr, 29t—Michael Callan. 7bm, 7br, 7c, 7ctl, 7ct, 7ctr, 8l, 12 both, 13 both, 14tr, 14c, 15, 19br, 24mr, 26bl, 28, 31tr, 31br, 34l, 34r, 36ml, 36bl, 37b, 38bl, 38br, 39r, 39bl, 43tl, 46mr, 48br, 50bl, 51 all, 52b, 53tl, 53c, 53br, 54, 56, 60b, 61b, 69c, 70c, 71tr, 71br, 73bl, 73tm, 76c—Digital Stock. 7ml, 39mtl—Jurgen and Christine Sohns/FLPA—Images of Nature. 7cb, 16b, 17br, 18ml, 20br, 22mr, 24br, 25ml, 26t, 29br, 31c, 46t, 48br, 49tl, 49mr, 73tl, 73mr—Stockbyte. 9c, 9mb, 35r, 55l, 57 both, 63mr—Royalty Free/CORBIS. 11c—Wolfgang Kaehler/CORBIS. 11br—Nick Garbutt/BBC Natural History Unit. 20bl—Roger Tidman/CORBIS. 21tr—RSPB Images. 21br, 61mr—Hubert Stadler/CORBIS. 21mr, 23tr—Brian Hunter Smart. 23br—Roger Tidman/FLPA—Images of Nature. 24l—Steve Kaufman/CORBIS. 26c—Yossi Eshbol/FLPA—Images of Nature. 27, 65t—Peter Oxford/BBC Natural History Unit. FLPA/CORBIS. 29ml—Doug Allen/BBC Natural History Unit. 32c—Michael & Patricia Fogden/CORBIS. 32mt, 34c—Anup Shah/BBC Natural History Unit. 35t, 42bl—Kevin Schafer/CORBIS. 39mtr, 41mr, 42ml, 42br—David Hosking/FLPA—Images of Nature. 41tl—Chris Hellier/BBC Natural History Unit. 43br—J.Tinning/FLPA—Images of Nature. 45mr—Charles Philip Cangialosi/CORBIS. 45tm—Keith Scholey/BBC Natural History Unit. 49bl, 55tl—Darrell Gulin/CORBIS. 51r—Thomas Lazar. 58mr, 74b—Mark Newman/FLPA—Images of Nature. 59tr—Michael Hollings/FLPA—Images of Nature. 61ml—Panda Photo/FLPA—Images of Nature. 61t—George Lepp/BBC Natural History Unit. 64t—Jim Clare/BBC Natural History Unit. 64br—Derk Hall/FLPA—Images of Nature. 65mr, 75c—Martin B. Withers/FLPA—Images of Nature. 66bm—Jeff Rotman/BBC Natural History Unit. 69mr—Dennis Degnan/CORBIS. 71ml—Foto Natura Stock/FLPA—Images of Nature. 72—Jeffrey L. Rottman/CORBIS. 74c, 75tr—Tom and Pam Gardner/FLPA—Images of Nature. 30 both, 33b, 77—Lynn M. Stone/BBC Natural History Unit.